KT-478-511

£27.50
neff

The Counties and Regions of the UK

The Counties and Regions of the UK

Economic, Industrial and Social Trends in Local Authority Areas

University of Warwick Business Information Service

Gower

© University of Warwick Business Information Service 1988.

All rights reserved. No part of this publication may be reproduced, stored in a retrieval system, or transmitted in any form or by any means, electronic, mechanical, photocopying, recording, or otherwise without the prior permission of Gower Publishing Company Limited.

Published by
Gower Publishing Company Limited,
Gower House,
Croft Road,
Aldershot
Hants GU11 3HR,
England

Gower Publishing Company,
Old Post Road,
Brookfield,
Vermont 05036,
USA

British Library Cataloguing in Publication Data

The Counties and regions of the UK: economic, industrial and social trends in local
    authority areas.
    1. Great Britain. Economic conditions – For businessmen
    I. University of Warwick. *Business Information Service* II. Mort, D. (David),
    330.941'0858

Library of Congress Cataloging-in-Publication Data

The Counties and regions of the UK.
    Rev. ed. of: The counties and regions of the U.K./David Mort. 1983.
    Bibliography: p.
    1. Great Britain—Economic conditions—1945-
I. Mort, D. Counties and regions of the U.K.
II. University of Warwick. Business Information Service.
HC256.6.M68   1988   330.941'085   888–1203

ISBN 0 566 02755 0

Printed in Great Britain at the University Press, Cambridge

Contents

The University of Warwick Business Information Service

The University of Warwick Business Information Service is a commercial information service based in the University Library. It was established over 10 years ago and provides statistical, market and business information to companies and other organizations. The service is based on a comprehensive international collection of statistical and market research data.

In addition to the enquiry service, the Business Information Service organizes a regular programme of seminars and is involved in a series of research projects. It has published a number of reviews and directories, the latest of which is *Sources of Unofficial UK Statistics* published by Gower in 1986.

The Centre for Local Economic Strategies

The Centre for Local Economic Strategies (CLES) is an independent organization established in 1985 offering research and information services on local economic development and policies. The CLES database contains publications from over 200 local authorities, supplemented by material from other organizations such as central government, academic organizations, research institutes, trade unions, employers' organizations, voluntary and community groups etc. Current awareness and enquiry services and regular seminar and publications programmes are available to local authorities and other interested organizations on a fee-paying basis.

Foreword

In 1983 Warwick Statistics Service (now renamed University of Warwick Business Information Service) published a review, 'The Counties & Regions of the UK'. The aim of this first edition was to give an overview of each local authority area and to pick out the salient factors – population, employment, etc. – from which a profile of the area could be built up. This review attracted considerable interest and was used in a number of different contexts, for example, in planning local sales and marketing campaigns and in local economic planning.

Since 1983 there have been considerable changes to the structure of local authorities, particularly with the abolition of the metropolitan counties and the Greater London Council. In addition, as local authorities have become more involved in economic development, more information has become available. All these changes have been incorporated in this revised and extended second edition.

The new edition includes broadly the same data as the first edition but has been extended by the addition of supplementary data on rateable value, local authority expenditure and initiatives and economic development costs. Time series have also been included for the first time.

This new edition was compiled by David Mort (who compiled the first edition), Information Officer for the Centre for Local Economic Strategies (and formerly Manager of Warwick Statistics Service), with the assistance of Christine Stanhope.

Introduction

This review outlines the main demographic, economic, industrial and employment trends in the fifty-four counties of England and Wales, the twelve regional and island areas of Scotland, and Northern Ireland and its districts. It updates the first edition produced in 1983. The United Kingdom as a whole has experienced the effect of both recession and growth in recent years, but these have affected different local areas in different ways. By looking at basic trends in population, employment, construction, and industrial development the review provides a guide to each area which will be of particular interest to those involved in business planning and marketing and those concerned with local economic planning and research.

Key statistics on population trends and characteristics, district sizes, unemployment, earnings, housing completions, industrial floorspace, industrial establishments by size bands, rateable value and local authority expenditure are given for each area, accompanied by a commentary. The commentary provides general information, outlines local employment and industry and includes a note on local authority initiatives to support the local economy. Details of specific developments such as new towns, enterprise zones, freeports and science parks are also included. Where possible, a series of figures are given for each key statistic covering the years from 1981 to the present time.

Information has been collected from various sources including central government statistics, local authorities, development agencies, professional bodies and private research organizations. A broad outline of the main sources used is given in the following section and these and other sources consulted are listed in the Bibliography at the end of the report. The figures contained in this report are intended only as a general guide to an area – more detailed information is available from the original sources noted.

Finally, I would like to thank all those organizations who have allowed us to use extracts of their information for this report. Of particular help have been various central government departments, notably OPCS, Department of Employment and the Department of the Environment, many local authorities, the Chartered Institute of Public Finance and Accountancy (CIPFA) and Market Location Ltd.

David Mort

While every effort has been made to ensure the accuracy of the contents, the compilers cannot accept any responsibility for any errors or omissions which may have occurred.

The Statistics

Population: Figures at June of year.

Unemployment rates: Various changes have been made to the methods of collecting and analysing the figures since 1979, making comparisons between 1987 and earlier years difficult. In Surrey and Warwickshire there are difficulties in defining the local unemployment areas, so for certain years, marked #, no figures are available. Figures at February of year.

Average earnings: Average weekly earnings of individuals surveyed in April each year.

Housing completions: Total completions (public and private). Where the county figure was not available, an estimate has been made by totalling up the district figures. These figures are marked with a † in the tables. Regular revised figures are produced – see issues of *Local Housing Statistics*. Only the first nine months' figures for 1986 were available when this report was prepared.

Employment: Industrial establishments identified at February 1987 covering Standard Industrial Classification (SICs) A–Z. The 'Employee %' figures show the percentage of establishments with fewer than 100 employees (–100), establishments with more than 100 but fewer than 1,000 (100+), establishments with more than a thousand (1,000+). For many counties the number of employees for some establishments was not known – these have been excluded from the percentages, which in these cases do not add up to 100.

Sources Used

Total population, district data, age structure: Data from the Office of Population, Censuses and Surveys (OPCS), General Register Office, Scotland and Northern Ireland Office. Main source used:
OPCS Monitor PP1: Mid 1985 Population Estimates for Local Government and Health Authority Areas.

A list of the main population series giving local area data is given in the Bibliography.

Unemployment rates: Data from monthly issues of the *Employment Gazette*, produced by the Department of Employment and available through HMSO.

Average earnings: Data from the *New Earnings Survey, Part E-1986*, available through HMSO.

Housing completions: Data from *Local Housing Statistics (England and Wales)* and *Scottish Housing Statistics (Scotland)*, both available through HMSO.

Industrial floorspace: Data from *Commercial and Industrial Floorspace Statistics, England* and *Commercial and Industrial Floorspace Statistics, Wales*. The former is no longer published but the last issue is available through HMSO, and the latter through the Welsh Office.

Industrial units and employment bands: Data from *Great Britain Industrial Statistics, Employee Analysis*, published twice a year by Market Location Limited. This lists units by size and employment band for each county area. It is aggregate data based on Market Location's census of UK industrial establishments. Their files contain a range of data on individual establishments which is used particularly for sales prospecting and market penetration studies for individual clients. An associate company is SAMI, offering retailing data on main shopping centres. Market Location files are also available online through Pergamon. Further information from Jackie Knightley, Market Location Ltd, 17 Waterloo Place, Warwick Street, Leamington Spa, CV32 5LA.

Rateable value, local authority expenditure: Data from *Local Government Comparative Statistics, Finance and General Statistics* and *Rating Review Estimates of Income and Expenditure, Summary Volume* published by the Chartered Institute of Public Finance and Accountancy (CIPFA). The Statistical Information Service (SIS) of CIPFA publishes a range of statistical titles on various local authority services and activities. For further details contact CIPFA, 3 Robert Street, London, WC2N 6BR.

The text: The text for each county and region area quotes data from the above sources plus various local authority reports listed in the Bibliography.

England

England

AVON

Total Population ('000)				1981 929.1		1984 939.8		1985 942.0	

Main Districts	1981	1984	1985
Bristol	401.3	396.6	393.8
Kingswood	84.6	86.8	87.9
Northavon	118.9	123.1	124.1
Woodspring	162.8	170.6	173.9

Age Structure 1985 ('000)	0–4 56.3	5–14 114.0	15–29 225.0	30–44 189.2	45–59/64 179.9	60/65–74 112.6	75+ 65.0

Unemployment Rates %	1981 8.6	1984 11.2	1985 11.7	1987 10.5

Average Earnings	1981	1984	1985	1986
Male	140.9	177.0	192.3	207.6
Female	90.3	112.8	124.4	134.2

Housing Completions	1981 3,288*	1984 2,968	1985 2,820	1986 2,689*†

Industrial Floorspace ('000 sq. metres)	1981 4,041.6	1984 4,066.6	1985 4,079.3

Employment
Industrial Establishments 1987 = 3,686

Employees %	–100 81.3	100+ 6.6	1,000+ 0.4

Rateable Value 1985 £m.	Total 126.502	Domestic % 51.8	Commercial % 24.7	Industrial % 8.5	Other % 14.9

Local Authority Expenditure (£'000)	83/84 359,140	84/85 356,949	86/87 417,869e

Economic Development Cost per capita (£)	82/83 0.14	84/85 0.14	85/86 0.15e

* Total of district figures
† Only 9 months' figures available for 1986
e Estimate
For notes on statistics see p. xi

Avon

Covering an area of 134,613 hectares, Avon is the most densely populated county in the South West, with Bristol as the main centre. A feature of the economy in recent years has been the growth of high technology industries and the office sectors. Traditional industries include aerospace, food, drink and tobacco and paper, printing and publishing. The county is at the western end of the so-called 'M4 Corridor' and has good transport links with the rest of the country.

Industry and Employment

The county has not suffered from the recession to the same extent as the national economy, although, at 405,000, the number employed in the area by 1985 was considerably smaller than that five years earlier. Employment is expected to rise only gradually and by 1990 is unlikely to have climbed above 425,000, a level not very different from that in 1979.

The relative prosperity of the local economy is partly accounted for by the high proportion of jobs in the nationally expanding service sector. Much of the recent growth has been in private services – for example, the relocation to Avon from London of important insurance firms has had a great influence on employment trends. The other major growth area has been jobs in leisure related activities. This new work in services, however, has not fully made up for the loss of more traditional types of employment. Women have taken the vast majority of these new jobs, often on a part-time basis. In contrast, jobs lost have often been full-time, occupied by males.

Employment in manufacturing has fallen by over a quarter to 100,000 in the last ten years, although the absence of major national industries in decline has limited this fall. The continuing prosperity of the large local aerospace industry, linked to the defence industry, has also cushioned the area from the recession. Around 20,000 are employed in the industry. High-technology industries have created about 1,500 jobs in the last few years and jobs expected over the remainder of the decade number 2,000. The local structure plan identifies substantial areas of land for industrial development particularly in Northern Bristol, Weston-super-Mare and Bath.

Changes in the economic structure of the county have also produced changes in the socio-economic structure. There is a higher proportion of employers and managers, professional workers and clerical and administration staff than the national average and a greater dominance of those social classes covering professional, intermediate and skilled non-manual occupations: 43.9 per cent compared with the national figure of 38.6 per cent.

Unemployment at February 1987 was 10.5 per cent, covering 44,078 people, although this hides the fact that inner city areas in Bristol, for example, are well above the national average.

Local Authority Initiatives

The County Council has an Economic Development Group which publishes various economic/industrial reviews of the area.
See: *Avon Economic Review*, published by EDG, April 1985.
Contact: Mr V. J. Robinson, PO Box 46, Avon House, North Bristol, BS99 7EU.
Bristol also has an Economic Development Department.

New Town

Bradley Stoke is the largest privately funded new town in Europe. Work has just started on this project to provide houses for 25,000 people near Bristol.

BEDFORDSHIRE

Total Population ('000)	1981	1984	1985
	510.3	515.7	516.7

Main Districts

	1981	1984	1985
North Bedfordshire	133.5	133.5	133.9
Luton	164.8	165.5	166.1
Mid-Bedfordshire	104.5	107.8	108.1
South Bedfordshire	107.5	109.0	108.6

Age Structure 1985 ('000)	0-4	5-14	15-29	30-44	45-59/64	60/65-74	75+
	37.1	71.8	127.6	110.5	96.2	48.7	24.8

Unemployment Rates %	1981	1984	1985	1987
	7.5	10.5	10.7	10.2

Average Earnings	1981	1984	1985	1986
Male	138.4	183.0	202.9	213.5
Female	90.5	115.1	123.9	131.0

Housing Completions	1981	1984	1985	1986
	1,952*	2,053	2,749*	1,269*†

Industrial Floorspace ('000 sq. metres)	1981	1984	1985
	2,925.6	2,926.5	2,912.4

Employment

Industrial Establishments	1987 = 1,331		
Employees %	-100	100+	1,000+
	78.5	8.8	0.8

Rateable Value 1985 £m.	Total	Domestic %	Commercial %	Industrial %	Other %
	88.244	49.3	22.4	15.4	13.0

Local Authority Expenditure (£'000)	83/84	84/85	86/87
	221,263	215,590	235,616e

Economic Development Cost per capita (£)	82/83	84/85	85/86
	0.07	0.43	0.39e

* Total of district figures
† Only 9 months' figures available for 1986
e Estimate
For notes on statistics see p. xi

The county covers 123,465 hectares to the north of Greater London. Employment is mainly in manufacturing, particularly engineering and vehicle manufacture, around the towns of Luton and Dunstable. In recent years there has been a considerable amount of new housing, office and shopping development, and mineral working and agriculture are also important in a county with a large number of rural areas. Warehousing and distribution is becoming increasingly significant. North–South road communications are good, with Bedford close to the M1, and the M25 orbital motorway is improving access to the South East. Luton Airport is important for charter flights and Stansted and Heathrow are close by.

Industry and Employment

Because of its strong manufacturing base the county experiences unemployment levels higher than most other areas in the South East, and in view of rising unemployment the County Structure Plan, approved in 1980, has been reviewed. Originally Bedfordshire sought to use its housing policies to generate growth – in the original plan over 30 per cent of the housing provision was to be located in the Luton/Dunstable area, the main employment centre in the county. In the proposed alterations Bedfordshire estimated that there would be a need for a further 41,000 jobs by 1996, with over a third expected in the Luton area. Therefore, the provisions for industry and commerce, largely restrained before, were significantly increased, with a quarter of the industry provision and half of the office provision being allocated to the Luton area. Originally 225 hectares had been allocated for industry and 12.5 hectares for offices – the revised level is 42.3 hectares for industry and 291,500 sq. metres for offices.

It is estimated that by 1991 housing policies could result in a population of 570,000 with 288,000 people actively seeking work.

The county has been relatively successful with new businesses – according to VAT returns 1,843 new businesses registered in the county between 1979 and 1983, a rise of 18 per cent, the third highest of the twelve counties in the South East.

The unemployment rate in February 1987 was 10.2 per cent, representing 22,391, but despite these levels there are general skill shortages.

Local Authority Initiatives

The work of the Council has largely involved the provision of sites for industrial development and offering advice/information largely through BECENTA – the Bedfordshire and Chilterns Enterprise Agency.

See: *Economic Development – A Policy Review*, published by the Employment Committee, November 1985.

Contact: A. M. Griffin, County Planning Officer, County Hall, Bedford, MK42 9AP.

BERKSHIRE

Total Population ('000)	1981	1984	1985
	693.8	715.3	724.0

Main Districts

Newbury	123.6	127.6	130.6
Reading	137.4	136.4	135.3
Slough	97.7	98.5	98.6
Windsor/Maidenhead	133.4	133.8	133.4
Wokingham	117.0	129.7	135.4

Age Structure 1985 ('000)	0–4	5–14	15–29	30–44	45–59/64	60/65–74	75+
	49.2	95.4	187.8	156.3	132.0	67.9	35.4

Unemployment Rates %	1981	1984	1985	1987
	5.9	7.4	7.6	6.5

Average Earnings	1981	1984	1985	1986
Male	153.5	196.8	212.2	238.6
Female	96.6	127.6	138.8	152.3

Housing Completions	1981	1984	1985	1986
	4,226*	5,638	3,735	2,637†

Industrial Floorspace ('000 sq. metres)	1981	1984	1985
	2,637.5	2,494.1	2,417.0

Employment

Industrial Establishments	1987 = 1,708		
Employees %	-100	100+	1,000+
	72.4	10.1	0.6

Rateable Value 1985 £m.	Total	Domestic %	Commercial %	Industrial %	Other %
	134.210	49.8	25.7	10.9	13.6

Local Authority Expenditure (£'000)	83/84	84/85	86/87
	261,803	x	293,427e

Economic Development Cost per capita (£)	82/83	84/85	85/86
	0.03	0.03	0.03e

* Total of district figures

† Only 9 months' figures available for 1986

e Estimate

x Figures not provided

For notes on statistics see p. xi

The county area is 125,940 hectares, situated to the west of Greater London. The River Thames flows through the county, which has rich arable and dairy farming land, while industrial development is largely concentrated around Reading, Slough and Bracknell New Town. The M4 cuts through the county and the M3 is nearby.

Industry and Employment

The area is experiencing a rapid rate of population growth. Between 1971 and 1981 there was a 7 per cent increase and estimates for 1985–1995 suggest a higher growth rate than this. OPCS give a 10.3 per cent rise while Cambridge Econometrics suggest a 9.5 per cent rise. Most of this rise will be due to natural growth, although migration also influences the age structure: the county generally gains migration – more move in than out – and migrants tend to be in the young adult age groups, with nearly half aged between 10 and 29 years. The revised Structure Plan anticipates the need for 40,500 new dwellings between 1984 and 1996. The county has a relatively small proportion of jobs in manufacturing, the sector hardest hit by the recession, so unemployment is well below the national average. There are strong service and distribution sectors and many new firms are new-technology-based – the electronics sector now accounts for 10 per cent of all employment within the county.

Originally there were three structure plans, for the east, central and west areas of the county. These have now been consolidated into one plan for the county which aims to limit new industrial, warehousing and office development so that it meets the growth anticipated in the local workforce and provides increased opportunities for the unemployed. The County Council believes that growth should no longer be concentrated in Central Berkshire but, in accordance with government guidance, should be directed to the East of London.

Unemployment at February 1987 was 6.5 per cent representing 21,107 people.

Local Authority Initiatives

Mainly limited to providing space for new firms.

See: *Economic Growth and Planning Policies in the South East*, published by Housing Research Foundation, November 1986.

Contact: Planning Department, Shire Hall, Shinfield Park, Reading, RG2 9XD.

New Town

Bracknell was designated in 1949. Original population: 5,149; present population (31 March 1984):51,600. At March 1984, 122 factories had been completed, covering 318,000 sq. metres of floorspace. 27,400 are employed in the town and the unemployment rate is 6.9 per cent. The Development Corporation was dissolved in 1982 and the administration is now with the Commission for the New Towns.

BUCKINGHAMSHIRE

Total Population		1981	1984	1985
('000)		571.8	594.6	601.6

Main Districts	1981	1984	1985
Aylesbury Vale	133.9	138.3	139.4
Chiltern	92.8	91.8	91.1
Milton Keynes	126.0	145.8	153.2
Wycombe	157.0	157.3	156.8

Age Structure 1985	0–4	5–14	15–29	30–44	45–59/64	60/65–74	75+
('000)	41.4	85.2	145.0	132.9	112.4	55.6	29.1

Unemployment Rates	1981	1984	1985	1987
%	7.0	9.4	8.7	7.7

Average Earnings	1981	1984	1985	1986
Male	139.3	181.1	197.3	218.9
Female	93.0	122.7	135.4	144.9

Housing Completions	1981	1984	1985	1986
	4,492*	5,186	3,904	2,960†

Industrial Floorspace	1981	1984	1985
('000 sq. metres)	2,176.1	2,225.6	2,213.5

Employment			
Industrial Establishments	1987 = 2,166		
Employees %	–100	100+	1,000+
	70.5	8.8	0.2

Rateable Value 1985	Total	Domestic %	Commercial %	Industrial %	Other %
£m.	106.354	56.3	21.8	10.8	11.0

Local Authority Expenditure	83/84	84/85	86/87
(£'000)	216,136	227,427	276,191e

Economic Development Cost per capita (£)	82/83	84/85	85/86
	0.05	0.01	0.02e

* Total of district figures

† Only 9 months' figures available for 1986

e Estimate

For notes on statistics see p. xi

Buckinghamshire covers 188,289 hectares to the north west of Greater London, and was the fastest growing county in terms of population between 1971 and 1981, largely due to the development of the new city of Milton Keynes. Elsewhere the county is largely rural in character – on the southern edge of the county lie the Chilterns, a nationally designated Area of Outstanding Natural Beauty.

Industry and Employment

Largely due to the growth of Milton Keynes, the county has developed strong distribution and service sectors. Services account for approximately 67 per cent of total employment. Aylesbury and High Wycombe are other major towns where a large percentage of the population commutes to London.

The Structure Plan does not quantify the levels of provision for industrial development and employment in the county but aims to concentrate new urban development into a few centres, notably Milton Keynes. This is to encourage a close geographical relationship between homes and jobs in north and mid-Bucks. It also discourages any development in the south of the county, where industrial and commercial development will be permitted only if it is consistent with the need of the locally resident population. The effect of this is to restrain development in High Wycombe, Chesham, and Amersham, with fewer restrictions in Aylesbury and Buckingham. The revised housing forecast now suggests that, between 1981 and 1991, 39,300 to 43,900 new homes will be needed, again largely in north and mid-Bucks. Population of the area is expected to rise by approximately 14 per cent between 1985 and 1995.

Unemployment at February 1987 was 7.7 per cent, representing 17,662 people.

Local Authority Initiatives

The County Council has had only a limited role in economic development, apart from structure plan restraints on growth etc.

See: *Economic Growth and Planning Policies in the South East*, published by Housing Research Foundation, November 1986.

Contact: Planning Department, County Offices, Aylesbury.

New Town

Milton Keynes was designated in 1967. Original population: 40,000; present population (31 March 1986): 128,400. At March 1986, 43,300 people were employed in the town and industrial floorspace covered 1,393,698 sq. metres. It achieved the highest population growth in Britain between 1971 and 1981, increasing its population by 102 per cent, and the total housing stock is now 48,283 dwellings. The Development Corporation has been relatively successful in attracting new companies and the target date for its wind up is 1992. The latest report from the town suggests that it is at the halfway stage of its development, with 60–70 per cent of the city still to be developed.

CAMBRIDGESHIRE

Total Population		1981	1984	1985	
('000)		591.4	609.2	621.4	

Main Districts

Cambridge		101.0	99.6	98.7	
Fenland		67.7	68.5	68.9	
Huntingdon		124.9	131.1	137.3	
Peterborough		134.3	141.2	144.6	
South Cambridgeshire		109.6	113.6	115.0	

Age Structure 1985	0–4	5–14	15–29	30–44	45–59/64	60/65–74	75+
('000)	40.9	83.9	155.7	130.2	110.9	64.5	35.3

Unemployment Rates	1981	1984	1985	1987
%	7.8	10.6	10.2	9.3

Average Earnings	1981	1984	1985	1986
Male	139.1	173.9	185.8	201.7
Female	87.3	113.8	118.6	133.6

Housing Completions	1981	1984	1985	1986
	4,087*	4,340	4,694	2,871†

Industrial Floorspace	1981	1984	1985
('000 sq. metres)	2,448.2	2,430.2	2,420.6

Employment

Industrial Establishments	1987 = 1,521		
Employees %	–100	100+	1,000+
	75.8	10.0	0.5

Rateable Value 1985	Total	Domestic %	Commercial %	Industrial %	Other %
£m.	91.996	51.7	21.4	10.2	16.6

Local Authority Expenditure	83/84	84/85	86/87
(£'000)	224,996	x	261,131e

Economic Development Cost	82/83	84/85	85/86
per capita (£)			
	0.31	0.41	0.44e

* Total of district figures

† Only 9 months' figures available for 1986

e Estimate

x Figures not provided

For notes on statistics see p. xi

Cambridgeshire is a largely rural county covering 340,914 hectares in East Anglia. The main settlements are Cambridge, Peterborough and Huntingdon, and most of the commercial and industrial growth has been in the western half of the county.

Industry and Employment

Although the county has experienced growth in recent years most of this has centred around Cambridge, and some of the outer agricultural areas, notably North Cambridgeshire, are suffering severe unemployment. Services have continued to increase their share of employment, now accounting for 66 per cent, with manufacturing declining at approximately 28 per cent.

The growth of new-technology industries in the Cambridge area has been particularly evident recently. A recent study identified 300 high-technology firms in the Cambridge area, and they are growing at a rate of approximately thirty new firms per year. Some labour shortages are now developing in this sector. Its proximity to London also makes Cambridge attractive and the development of Stansted in nearby Essex will bring international airport facilities close. Peterborough has also attracted new industry, particularly services, but it still has some way to go to counterbalance the losses it has suffered in heavy engineering, and in some parts of the city unemployment is well over 20 per cent.

Between now and the end of the century the population is expected to rise by 100,444 from the present 650,000, generating demand for 55,000 new houses. Cambridge's tight boundaries have prevented large new housing developments but considerable growth is taking place in the villages around the city.

The Structure Plan, now being revised, will maintain restrictions on new housing and shopping provision in Cambridge itself, stimulate job growth and maintain services in the north and east of the county, and apply some restraint on job growth in the south and west. High-technology industry will be encouraged in the Cambridge–Huntingdon–Peterborough corridor and other industry will be encouraged elsewhere, particularly to help diversify the economic base of the Fens.

Unemployment in February 1987 was 9.3 per cent, representing 23,970 people.

Local Authority Initiatives

Two thirds of the County Council's Economic Development budget assists District Councils to open up land for industry and provide small factory units. Over 75 per cent of the budget is spent in the north east. The Wisbech/Ramsay/Soham area has been designated a Rural Development Area.

See: *East Anglia Regional Commentary 1985/86*, published by East Anglia Consultative Committee, March 1986.

Contact: Mr R. Brown, Planning and Research, Shire Hall, Castle Hill, Cambridge, CB3 0AP.

New Towns

Peterborough was designated in 1967. Original population: 81,000; present population (31 March 1986): 130,520. Employment in the town is now 71,620 and industrial floorspace covers 1,161,729 sq. metres. The corporation's target wind up date is September 1988 and there is a target to create 2,000 jobs in the time left.

Bar Hill is a private new town development five miles from Cambridge, established in 1965 and covering 142 hectares with a population of 3,220. Planned population is 4,200.

Science Parks

Cambridge Science Park was established in 1972 by Trinity College and eight other tenant companies with ground leases. Three phases of development have been completed and 68 occupiers are now on sites covering 530,000 sq. ft of floorspace. Another phase is being developed and a further phase is in preparation.

St John's Innovation Centre opened in 1987.

CHESHIRE

Total Population ('000)				1981	1984	1985	
				932.6	937.4	942.4	

Main Districts							
Chester				116.3	116.4	116.6	
Halton				123.2	122.7	122.9	
Macclesfield				149.9	150.2	151.5	
Vale Royal				112.1	112.5	113.5	
Warrington				169.8	175.9	177.5	

Age Structure 1985 ('000)	0–4	5–14	15–29	30–44	45–59/64	60/65–74	75+
	59.8	128.1	218.3	197.0	184.9	102.8	51.5

Unemployment Rates %	1981	1984	1985	1987
	10.7	13.9	13.7	12.8

Average Earnings	1981	1984	1985	1986
Male	141.3	185.0	200.5	210.9
Female	89.9	113.2	124.1	132.8

Housing Completions	1981	1984	1985	1986
	2,961*	4,342	3,350	2,177†

Industrial Floorspace ('000 sq. metres)	1981	1984	1985
	5,675.8	5,718.3	5,655.2

Employment			
Industrial Establishments	1987 = 1,568		
Employees %	–100	100+	1,000+
	61.5	10.2	0.6

Rateable Value 1985 £m.	Total	Domestic %	Commercial %	Industrial %	Other %
	142.048	50.7	17.2	16.4	15.7

Local Authority Expenditure (£'000)	83/84	84/85	86/87
	393,528	377,150	428,684e

Economic Development Cost per capita (£)	82/83	84/85	85/86
	1.02	0.87	0.94e

* Total of district figures

† Only 9 months' figures available for 1986

e Estimate

For notes on statistics see p. xi

Cheshire

A county of 232,850 hectares to the south of Merseyside and Manchester conurbations, Cheshire is well known for its brine and building and silica sand deposits, and there are also large areas of agricultural land. There is a significant industrial belt to the north of the county which includes the chemical towns of Widnes and Runcorn and two new town developments at Warrington and Runcorn.

Industry and Employment

The population has increased steadily over the last two decades. Between 1971 and 1981 there was an increase of 6.7 per cent and from 1981 to 1985 a further increase of 0.5 per cent. County Council forecasts suggest a rise to 956,200 by 1988 and a further rise to 970,000 by 1991. During the last fifteen years the main growth area has been Halton District – here the population has increased by 27 per cent due to the build up of Runcorn New Town.

Manufacturing accounts for approximately 33 per cent of employment and the chemicals, vehicles and construction industries are particularly well represented in terms of employment. One of the county's natural resources, salt, has formed the basis for an inorganic chemicals industry which has led to the growth of pharmaceuticals and petrochemicals industries. A recent diversification in the local economy has been the growth of the brewing industry in Runcorn and Warrington. A number of research establishments are also located in the county including Risley Materials Laboratory, the European Space Tribology Centre, Jodrell Bank and a UK Atomic Energy Complex.

Unemployment at February 1987 was 12.8 per cent, representing 51,020 people.

Local Authority Initiatives

Concentrate on the development of new firms/businesses.

See: *Cheshire Current Facts and Figures*, monthly. Published by Research and Intelligence, County Council.

Contact: Employment Promotion Officer, Commerce House, Hunter Street, Chester, CH1 1SN.

New Towns

Runcorn was designated in 1964. Original population: 28,500; present population (31 March 1986): 67,500. The town is administered jointly with Warrington New Town, below. Industrial floorspace at March 1986 covered 440,742 sq. metres and there were 16,491 dwellings in the town.

Warrington was designated in 1968. Original population: 122,300; present population (31 March 1986): 143,500. The town is administered jointly with Runcorn New Town. Industrial floorspace covers 417,914 sq. metres and there are 10,213 dwellings in the town.

CLEVELAND

Total Population ('000)	1981	1984	1985
	570.3	562.7	559.9

Main Districts			
Hartlepool	94.9	92.4	91.6
Langbaurgh	150.9	148.9	147.7
Middlesbrough	150.6	146.9	144.8
Stockton-on-Tees	173.9	174.5	175.8

Age Structure 1985 ('000)	0–4	5–14	15–29	30–44	45–59/64	60/65–74	75+
	40.1	78.9	136.9	111.5	108.4	57.8	26.3

Unemployment Rates %	1981	1984	1985	1987
	16.6	20.6	22.8	20.8

Average Earnings	1981	1984	1985	1986
Male	140.9	174.7	187.8	199.5
Female	89.1	109.8	121.7	–

Housing Completions	1981	1984	1985	1986
	1,939	2,134	1,487*	1,085†

Industrial Floorspace ('000 sq. metres)	1981	1984	1985
	2,071.3	1,958.9	1,919.3

Employment			
Industrial Establishments	1987 = 982		
Employees %	–100	100+	1,000+
	80.1	9.8	0.8

Rateable Value 1985 £m.	Total	Domestic %	Commercial %	Industrial %	Other %
	81.354	42.1	15.8	23.6	18.5

Local Authority Expenditure (£'000)	83/84	84/85	86/87
	275,730	x	311,347e

Economic Development Cost per capita (£)	82/83	84/85	85/86
	2.83	2.19	2.76e

– Figures not available
* Total of district figures
† Only 9 months' figures available for 1986
e Estimate
x Figures not provided
For notes on statistics see p. xi

Cleveland

Situated in the North East of England and covering 58,310 hectares, Cleveland is one of the smallest counties in the country but has a number of large urban industrial areas particularly around Middlesbrough, Hartlepool, Billingham and Stockton. The area has been dependent on traditional industries such as iron and steel, shipbuilding and heavy engineering, and it also has the largest petrochemical complex in Europe. Teesside is the third most important part of Britain, and the country has a number of rural areas, including part of the North Yorks Moors National Park.

Industry and Employment

The County Council estimates that 182,400 people were in employment in 1984, a decrease of 52,100 between 1978 and 1984. Reliance on traditional industries, notably steel, has led to drastic cuts in employment levels. Between 1981 and 1984, for example, the following job losses were recorded: steel industry – 7,000; chemicals – 3,500; heavy engineering and shipbuilding – 2,000. Construction industry employment appears to have bottomed out and may increase slightly. There has been a shift in the area's industrial structure from manufacturing to services but this is mainly due to a fall in manufacturing employment rather than through any real rise in service employment.

It is anticipated that the county's total population figure of 564,300 in 1985 will change very little up to 1991, and only a marginal increase in employment is anticipated in the same period. The amount of net outward migration is projected to average about 2,400 per annum up to 1989.

The official unemployment rate in the county exceeds that for any county in Britain and Northern Ireland and long term unemployment has increased dramatically. In February 1987, 51,479 people were unemployed, a rate of 20.8 per cent.

Local Authority Initiatives

The Council has been active in developing a range of initiatives including support for the development of indigenous industry, inward investment, training initiatives, new technology strategies, and corporate approaches responding to unemployment, deprivation etc. The Research and Intelligence section produces regular economic reviews, sector reports etc. The Council also has a database, *INDATA*, covering 2,000 products and services sold by Cleveland's industry, available for consultation and aimed at making the local economy more self sufficient.

See: *Cleveland Economic and Demographic Review, 1990*, published by Research and Intelligence, 1986.

Contact: R. D. Fox, Research and Intelligence, PO Box No. 17, Rede House, 67 Corporation Road, Middlesbrough, TS1 1LY.

New Town

Ingleby Barwick is a private new town development in Stockton-on-Tees. The planned population is 22,000.

Enterprise Zones

Two zones are based in the area: Hartlepool, designated in October 1981, and Middlesbrough, designated in November 1983. By 1985 Hartlepool had 73 establishments, employing 2,100 people, and Middlesbrough had 70, employing 700 people. Within the Middlesbrough zone is the Cleveland CADCAM Centre, the first of its kind in Europe, consisting of a computer and information centre on CADCAM development for industry.

CORNWALL

Total Population ('000)			1981	1984	1985	
			426.5	439.0	443.8	

Main Districts	1981	1984	1985
Caradon	67.7	71.4	72.5
Carrick	75.7	77.5	78.3
Kerries	83.6	86.0	85.8
North Cornwall	64.8	67.4	68.7
Restormel	78.6	80.1	81.2

Age Structure 1985 ('000)	0–4	5–14	15–29	30–44	45–59/64	60/65–74	75+
	25.6	54.8	91.6	85.3	89.0	61.9	35.6

Unemployment Rates %	1981	1984	1985	1987
	14.8	17.4	19.1	19.2

Average Earnings	1981	1984	1985	1986
Male	118.1	149.6	159.8	169.3
Female	82.3	103.0	109.7	119.4

Housing Completions	1981	1984	1985	1986
	1,610*	2,034*	2,138	1,946[†]

Industrial Floorspace ('000 sq. metres)	1981	1984	1985
	770.4	786.4	780.2

Employment			
Industrial Establishments	1987 = 560		
Employees %	−100	100+	1,000+
	78.8	8.1	

Rateable Value 1985 £m.	Total	Domestic %	Commercial %	Industrial %	Other %
	48.859	57.4	22.6	6.3	13.7

Local Authority Expenditure (£'000)	83/84	84/85	86/87
	152,834	158,057	181,171e

Economic Development Cost per capita (£)	82/83	84/85	85/86
	0.88	0.90	0.86e

* Total of district figures
† Only 9 months' figures available for 1986
e Estimate
For notes on statistics see p. xi

Cornwall is a rural county in the extreme south west of England. It is traditionally a mining and farming area and a tourist centre, with few large settlements. It covers an area of 354,662 hectares. Twenty-five miles south west of Land's End are the Isles of Scilly, over 200 islands and rocks, of which only five are inhabited.

Industry and Employment

Cornwall remains largely dependent for employment on its traditional industries such as farming, fishing and mining: industries whose labour requirements have declined in recent years. As a result job opportunities are limited, with a disproportionate importance placed on the service sector, particularly on distribution and catering. This sector includes tourism, which is important, employing 13 per cent of the workforce, but can also give rise to problems associated with its seasonal nature and low pay. Jobs in tourism have changed little since 1976.

In addition to the above, the county's problems are exacerbated by its remoteness, scattered communities and lack of infrastructure. For example, in 1981, 25 per cent of the population lived in communities of under 1,000 and 43 per cent in communities under 2,000. The population is also growing – in 1985 the population was approximately 440,000, a growth of 15.8 per cent since 1971, with the largest yearly increase being 7,000 in 1983–84. There is a particularly high retired population, representing approximately 19 per cent.

Cornwall's economy is characterized by small businesses: over half of the workforce is employed in firms with under 25 people. There is a large self-employed sector which accounts for some 21 per cent of the total workforce. Average earnings are extremely low and Cornwall consistently comes very near, if not at, the bottom of the league table of counties.

Unemployment in February 1987 was 19.2 per cent, covering 28,191 people. This is well above the national average, with variations between areas and between winter and summer. In local areas there is also often over-dependence on a single employer, which can have severe local effects if that source dwindles – South East Caradon, for example, is heavily dependent on Devonport Dockyard, where 2,000 jobs are being shed. The female activity rate is also well below the national average.

Local Authority Initiatives

For the last three years the Council has produced an annual review of its economic policies and programmes covering infrastructure improvements, industrial land provision, small business support, promotion etc. Regular bids are made to the EEC for funds and the County Council, in association with the Isles of Scilly and other local councils, has submitted a detailed Rural Development Programme to the Development Commission.

See: *Economic Policies and Programmes 1986*, published by the Planning and Employment Committee, 1986.

Contact: County Planning Officer, County Hall, Truro.

CUMBRIA

Total Population ('000)	1981 481.3	1984 483.6	1985 484.4			

Main Districts			
Allerdale	95.8	95.5	95.6
Barrow-in-Furness	73.5	74.0	74.1
Carlisle	101.6	101.4	101.3
Copeland	72.9	71.8	71.2
South Lakeland	94.9	96.8	97.4

Age Structure 1985 ('000)	0–4 28.5	5–14 60.5	15–29 108.8	30–44 96.0	45–59/64 96.3	60/65–74 61.2	75+ 33.1

Unemployment Rates %	1981 10.0	1984 11.5	1985 12.8	1987 12.1

Average Earnings	1981	1984	1985	1986
Male	134.7	168.6	180.0	133.7
Female	86.8	107.7	114.0	–

Housing Completions	1981 1,317*	1984 1,323*	1985 1,431	1986 1,121†

Industrial Floorspace ('000 sq. metres)	1981 2,027.3	1984 2,073.6	1985 2,046.9

Employment			
Industrial Establishments	1987 = 805		
Employees %	–100 80.7	100+ 9.8	1,000+ 0.9

Rateable Value 1985 £m.	Total 50.406	Domestic % 49.9	Commercial % 17.4	Industrial % 13.3	Other % 19.3

Local Authority Expenditure (£'000)	83/84 201,259	84/85 191,110	86/87 225,104e

Economic Development Cost per capita (£)	82/83 1.61	84/85 1.96	85/86 2.41e

* Total of district figures

† Only 9 months' figures available for 1986

e Estimate

For notes on statistics see p. xi

Cumbria covers 688,555 hectares, making it England's second largest county. There are industrial areas along the west coast and large tracts of agricultural and forested land. The Lake District National Park, a section of the Yorkshire Dales Park, Hadrian's Wall and the North Pennines are all in the county, which makes it an important tourist area. Major towns are Carlisle, Whitehaven, and the coastal town of Barrow.

Industry and Employment

In October 1986 it was estimated that there were 190,000 jobs in Cumbria; of these 164,700 were filled by employees and 25,000 were self-employed. About 30 per cent of jobs are in manufacturing, 57 per cent in services, 6 per cent in construction and 7 per cent in primary industries such as agriculture.

Overall it is estimated that the number of jobs provided by manufacturing will slowly decline over the next few years. However, this may not occur at the local level where individual firms can maintain or increase employment. Vickers, for example, is modernizing its Barrow shipyard to deal with new defence-related orders. Investment in a thermal oxide reprocessing plant at Sellafield will provide 3,000 jobs during construction. In the chemicals industry, employment is likely to expand as companies like Albright and Wilson and Glaxo expand capacity. Jobs have also been created in Barrow, the construction and onshore reception base for the Morecambe Bay gas field. Agricultural employment is falling slightly and forestry and mining-based employment is fairly stable with no great potential for growth.

Employment in the service sector is growing slightly and an important element in service spending is tourism. A 1986 Cumbria Tourist Board report concluded that 25,000 jobs are supported by direct and indirect visitor spending. Other service development is patchy – low incomes, scattered populations, and low accessibility all reduce the potential market for services.

The Structure Plan has identified 51 industrial sites in the area, totalling 218 hectares. There are still local shortages, particularly in Barrow, North Allerdale, South Copeland and in parts of Carlisle and South Lakeland. The Council is also encouraging the provision of sites for high-technology industry in West and South Cumbria.

Unemployment was 12.1 per cent at February 1987, representing 22,659 people.

Local Authority Initiatives

The Council has an Employment Development Strategy reviewed annually which includes the provision of sites, training initiatives, infrastructure improvements and the involvement of the local unions in industrial planning. Most of the county is also a Rural Development Area.

See: *Looking for Jobs – an Employment Development Strategy for Cumbria*, published by Economic Development Department, January 1987.

Contact: J. E. Burnet, Director, Economic Development, The Courts, Carlisle, CA3 8NA.

Cumbria

Enterprise Zone

Allerdale in Workington has had an enterprise zone since 4 October 1983. In 1985 there were 97 establishments in the zone, employing 1,400 people.

DERBYSHIRE

Total Population		1981	1984	1985
('000)		914.4	911.7	912.4

Main Districts	1981	1984	1985
Amber Valley	109.8	109.4	108.8
Chesterfield	96.7	97.2	96.8
Derby	217.4	214.7	215.3
Erewash	103.2	104.2	105.0
North East Derbyshire	97.5	96.3	97.0

Age Structure 1985	0–4	5–14	15–29	30–44	45–59/64	60/65–74	75+
('000)	56.1	118.1	204.0	187.3	180.4	109.4	57.1

Unemployment Rates	1981	1984	1985	1987
%	8.2	11.8	13.9	13.9

Average Earnings	1981	1984	1985	1986
Male	138.0	165.9	178.8	193.8
Female	86.7	108.8	116.1	125.4

Housing Completions	1981	1984	1985	1986
	3,106*	3,827	3,187	2,310*†

Industrial Floorspace	1981	1984	1985
('000 sq. metres)	5,875.3	6,053.8	5,924.1

Employment			
Industrial Establishments	1987 = 2,642		
Employees %	−100	100+	1,000+
	74.1	9.7	0.6

Rateable Value 1985	Total	Domestic %	Commercial %	Industrial %	Other %
£m.	109.163	52.5	16.4	15.3	15.8

Local Authority Expenditure	83/84	84/85	86/87
(£'000)	363,550	384,994	425,509e

Economic Development Cost per capita (£)	82/83	84/85	85/86
	0.45	0.42	0.91e

* Total of district figures
† Only 9 months' figures for 1986
e Estimate
For notes on statistics see p. xi

Derbyshire

Derbyshire covers 263,106 hectares and is situated in the centre of England between the cities of Manchester, Sheffield and Nottingham. The economy is varied, although metals, textiles, coal and quarrying are the major employers and it is these which have shed labour recently. Tourism – the Peak Park is in the north of the county – and public services provide important sources of employment. The M1 runs along the county's eastern boundary, and it is served by the inter-city railway between Sheffield and London.

Industry and Employment

Since the 1960s the population of the area has been increasing – in 1971 the population was 886,611 and in 1985 it was 912,400. Not all districts, however, have experienced growth. In the City of Derby there has been a decline primarily due to peripheral housing developments and a general outward movement of the population to small villages in adjacent areas. A June 1978 survey recorded 343,600 people working in the county, but since then there have been significant changes in employment levels. By December 1983 the employment level had fallen to 316,350 with varying changes at sectoral level. The greatest absolute loss occurred in textiles and clothing, with 8,000 losses. Manufacturing as a whole lost 30,000 jobs or 19 per cent of total jobs existing in 1978, but there were some offsetting increases in service employment, especially in professional services and health. In 1983 manufacturing accounted for 126,800 jobs, agriculture and energy for 26,400 and services for 163,150.

A further problem is that various localities are dominated in employment terms by declining industries, and job losses are not spread evenly across the county. The greatest loss was in Chesterfield (12.8 per cent) due to losses in the coal industry, while Derby lost 10.3 per cent with greatest absolute losses in the vehicle sector. South Derbyshire District, on the other hand, experienced a slight increase in employment (+0.9 per cent) due to expansion in coal-based employment and personal services.

A further hindrance to development has been the amount of derelict land in the county – in 1982 there was some 2,000 hectares of derelict land, of which 30 per cent was related to coalmining activity.

Unemployment in February 1987 was 50,344 people, a rate of 13.9 per cent.

Local Authority Initiatives

The County Council has been actively promoting economic development for a number of years and now has an industrial estate and advance factory building programme. It has created ITEC/Innovation Centres, Small Business Centres and the Derbyshire Cooperative Development Agency. It was also involved in establishing an Enterprise Board in late 1986.

See: *Economic Development in Shire Counties, Case Study 1 – Derby and Derbyshire*, published by CLES, 1987.

Contact: Planning Department, County Offices, Matlock, Derbyshire.

DEVON

Total Population ('000)	1981	1984	1985
	965.6	978.3	988.0

Main Districts			
East Devon	107.9	109.6	112.2
Exeter	99.8	100.8	99.7
Plymouth	252.9	255.3	253.4
Teignbridge	96.4	97.9	100.6
Torbay	113.1	115.1	117.9

Age Structure 1985 ('000)	0–4	5–14	15–29	30–44	45–59/64	60/65–74	75+
	55.6	116.1	220.0	184.7	185.5	138.5	87.6

Unemployment Rates %	1981	1984	1985	1987
	11.3	14.0	14.4	13.6

Average Earnings	1981	1984	1985	1986
Male	124.7	156.8	165.1	180.6
Female	84.9	108.3	115.6	129.1

Housing Completions	1981	1984	1985	1986
	2,677*	4,604*	4,781	3,482*†

Industrial Floorspace ('000 sq. metres)	1981	1984	1985
	2,145.3	2,154.0	2,157.7

Employment			
Industrial Establishments	1987 = 1,907		
Employees %	–100	100+	1,000+
	81.5	7.5	0.1

Rateable Value 1985 £m.	Total	Domestic %	Commercial %	Industrial %	Other %
	118.438	56.5	22.0	5.4	16.1

Local Authority Expenditure (£'000)	83/84	84/85	86/87
	334,433	349,536	401,342e

Economic Development Cost per capita (£)	82/83	84/85	85/86
	0.42	0.55	0.50e

* Total of district figures
† Only 9 months' figures available for 1986
e Estimate
For notes on statistics see p. xi

Devon

Its area of 671,099 hectares makes Devon the third largest county in England and Wales. Tourism and agriculture are the principal activities and the county has two national parks, Dartmoor and Exmoor. Mineral extraction is also an important activity. The main towns and cities are Exeter, Plymouth and Torquay.

Industry and Employment

The economic problems of Devon derive largely from its peripheral location in the UK. Its problems are low level of facilities, low density of population and low wage levels. Some areas of the county have a dispersed population, with poor infrastructure, particularly transport.

The people of Devon depend largely on the service sector to create jobs. This sector accounts for 60 per cent of employees, and is likely to offer the bulk of employment opportunities in the next five years. The second largest sector is manufacturing, with 21 per cent of jobs, although this sector's share has been declining in recent years. Since 1984 only a small part of the county has had Assisted Area status and this, coupled with the probable contraction in jobs at HM Dockyard, Devonport, will add to the difficulties in retaining manufacturing jobs.

Two smaller sectors are primary industries and construction, with approximately 10 per cent of employees. The economic effect on the county's economy, however, must not be underestimated. Agriculture, for example, directly employed 10,309 persons in 1981, apart from 12,700 farmers, and is also the basis of a thriving food-processing industry and a major customer of the service sector. Mining and quarrying, particularly ball and china clay extraction, are also important. The Structure Plan has identified five areas as having priority for development – Barnstaple, Exeter, Newton Abbot/Torbay, Plymouth and Tiverton/Cullompton/Willand.

In 1985, the average adult wage in Devon for full-time male employees was £27 less than in Great Britain as a whole and Devon's level of pay was 37th lowest of the 39 shire counties of England.

Unemployment in February 1987 was 13.6 per cent, representing 49,306 people.

Local Authority Initiatives

The County and Districts have active industrial promotion units and this activity is spearheaded by the Devon and Cornwall Development Bureau (DCDB), a government-backed development agency. The County has also established an employment fund of £1m for job creation, and supports tourist activities and co-operative development. Devon is also designated a Rural Development Area (RDA) by the Development Commission, and a three-year programme up to 1989 has been developed.

See: *Employment in Devon: Policies and Programmes*, published by Economy and Employment Committee, 1986, £2.

Contact: Engineering and Planning Department, Lucombe House, County Hall, Topsham Road, Exeter, EX2 4QW.

DORSET

Total Population ('000)			1981	1984	1985	
			598.6	617.8	627.7	

Main Districts						
Bournemouth			143.4	147.2	149.7	
Poole			120.3	122.7	124.5	
West Dorset			80.0	81.2	81.3	
Weymouth and Portland			58.0	59.7	60.9	
Wimborne			69.1	73.9	76.2	

Age Structure 1985 ('000)	0–4	5–14	15–29	30–44	45–59/64	60/65–74	75+
	32.9	68.9	133.1	113.5	119.7	96.5	63.1

Unemployment Rates %	1981	1984	1985	1987
	9.0	11.8	12.3	11.2

Average Earnings	1981	1984	1985	1986
Male	132.7	165.4	179.1	194.5
Female	83.4	109.6	118.0	126.3

Housing Completions	1981	1984	1985	1986
	3,848*	4,075	4,698	2,012*†

Industrial Floorspace ('000 sq. metres)	1981	1984	1985
	1,688.5	1,689.1	1,694.3

Employment			
Industrial Establishments	1987 = 1,153		
Employees %	–100	100+	1,000+
	70.7	7.0	0.6

Rateable Value 1985 £m.	Total	Domestic %	Commercial %	Industrial %	Other %
	89.840	59.8	21.4	6.1	12.7

Local Authority Expenditure (£'000)	83/84	84/85	86/87
	220,264	206,780	241,859e

Economic Development Cost per capita (£)	82/83	84/85	85/86
	0.04	0.04	0.04e

* Total of district figures
† Only 9 months' figures available for 1986
e Estimate
For notes on statistics see p. xi

Dorset

Dorset is a largely rural county covering 265,388 hectares. Agriculture is a major activity, although manufacturing and service centres exist, particularly around Poole, Christchurch and Weymouth. Tourism is another important part of the local economy.

Industry and Employment

The economy of Dorset is still characterized by its tourism and recreation industries, its strong personal service sector (including the retail trades) and, in the rural west and north, by agriculture and its related activities. During the last twenty years the service sector in South East Dorset has been further strengthened by the rapid development of office-based employment, particularly that relating to insurance, banking and finance. Between 1971 and 1981, total employment in service industries increased by 22,700 (19.8 per cent) and this was particularly marked in South East Dorset.

The Structure Plan for South East Dorset set a target of an increase of 32,500 jobs in the area between 1976 and 1996, and the plan added that manufacturing and warehousing should create 7,500 jobs and office-based employment 15,000 jobs. In the manufacturing sector, firms in the high-technology areas of computing and computer services, defence and marine electronics and aerospace are particularly well represented.

Dorset's population is growing. Between 1971 and 1981 it increased by almost 8 per cent and between 1981 and 1985 by a further 4.8 per cent. Some of the individual districts experienced greater growth than this, notably Poole with an 11 per cent growth between 1971 and 1981 and Wimborne with a 32 per cent growth in the same period. The population is forecast to increase to 637,000 in 1991, with a rise to 408,700 in South East Dorset and to 229,200 elsewhere in the county. Population of working age is forecast to increase by 8.5 per cent up to 1991 and the county is also a major recipient of retirement migration, which in turn generates a significant level of employment in supporting services.

Until recently Dorset was largely sheltered from the economic recession. In 1979 unemployment was only 4 per cent, but by February 1987 it had risen to 11.2 per cent, representing 25,016 people.

Local Authority Initiatives

The County Council has various schemes to assist industry including Dorset Enterprise Agency Schemes and schemes partly sponsored by the Development Commission. Part of West Dorset has been designated a Rural Development Area (RDA) and a three-year development programme has been produced.

See: *Dorset Data*, published by Planning Department, 1986.

Contact: Economic Development Officer, County Hall, Dorchester, DT1 1XJ.

DURHAM

Total Population ('000)		1981	1984	1985
		611.3	603.7	600.9

Main Districts	1981	1984	1985
Darlington	98.6	100.3	99.7
Derwentside	88.4	86.8	86.3
Durham	88.4	87.5	86.7
Easington	101.4	97.6	97.1
Sedgefield	93.5	89.9	89.3

Age Structure 1985 ('000)	0–4	5–14	15–29	30–44	45–59/64	60/65–74	75+
	37.0	77.0	137.1	121.2	121.1	71.7	35.8

Unemployment Rates %	1981	1984	1985	1987
	14.0	16.6	18.7	17.4

Average Earnings	1981	1984	1985	1986
Male	135.5	162.0	175.3	188.9
Female	88.1	109.0	118.2	127.8

Housing Completions	1981	1984	1985	1986
	1,700*	1,880	1,817	976*†

Industrial Floorspace ('000 sq. metres)	1981	1984	1985
	3,336.9	2,977.3	3,017.1

Employment			
Industrial Establishments	1987 = 886		
Employees %	–100	100+	1,000+
	67.9	12.7	0.9

Rateable Value 1985 £m.	Total	Domestic %	Commercial %	Industrial %	Other %
	60.155	50.8	17.7	11.9	19.6

Local Authority Expenditure (£'000)	83/84	84/85	86/87
	247,727	242,515	260,380e

Economic Development Cost per capita (£)	82/83	84/85	85/86
	0.77	0.72	1.08e

* Total of district figures
† Only 9 months' figures available for 1986
e Estimate
For notes on statistics see p. xi

Durham

A county of 243,597 hectares in the north east of England, Durham stretches from the Pennines in the west to the coast in the east and lies between industrial Tyneside to the north and Teesside in the south. Coalmining is the biggest activity, although declining, and other major industries include iron and steel and chemicals. The southern part of the county is mainly rural.

Industry and Employment

The main areas of employment are Derwentside, Durham City, Sedgefield and Darlington and all have suffered in recent years through the decline of traditional sectors, notably coal and steel. The steel works at Consett has also closed. Newer industries, particularly in high technology and food and drink, are moving into the area but a recent report from the County Council has noted that, between 1978 and 1983, 15,000 jobs have been lost in the county. To replace these job losses by 1988 would require a sixfold increase in the rate of new firm formation.

Manufacturing now accounts for approximately 27 per cent of employment, with services and construction combined providing 63.2 per cent, but the situation varies between areas. In Durham City services are becoming increasingly important, Sedgefield has probably the broadest economic base and Easington is now the only district where coalmining is a major industry – 10,000 people are still employed in the industry here, representing one third of the male workforce. The rural area of the Durham Dales has also suffered population and employment losses in recent years – in 1984, employment here stood at 4,650, a fall of 30 per cent since 1971, and a quarter of the population has been lost in the same period.

Unemployment at February 1987 was 17.4 per cent, representing 39,255 people.

Local Authority Initiatives

Financial aid and sites for industry plus area strategies, including those for employment creation and derelict land reclamation in the East Durham Coalfield and the regeneration of the Durham Dales.

See: *Manufacturing Employment Change in County Durham since 1965*, published by Planning Department, 1984.

Contact: Planning Department, County Hall, Durham, DH1 5UL.

New Towns

Aycliffe was designated in 1947. Original population: 60; present population (31 March 1986): 25,500. The Development Corporation has been extended to 1988. There are 177 companies in the town, employing 7,827 people. Housing stock covers 9,990 dwellings.

Peterlee was designated in 1948. Original population: 200; present population (31 March 1986): 24,000. The Development Corporation has been extended to 1988. In 1986, 6,759 people were employed in the town and the housing stock covered 9,664 dwellings.

Science Park

Mountjoy Research Centre, was established in Durham, by Durham University and English Estates, in October 1985. It covers 2.7 acres and had five companies on site at December 1986.

EAST SUSSEX

Total Population ('000)			1981 665.3	1984 678.9	1985 682.4	

Main Districts						
Brighton			149.4	145.6	143.1	
Hove			87.8	89.6	89.5	
Lewes			79.0	82.7	84.4	
Wealden			119.3	123.3	124.8	

Age Structure 1985 ('000)	0–4 35.7	5–14 71.6	15–29 139.9	30–44 123.0	45–59/64 126.2	60/65–74 107.7	75+ 78.3

Unemployment Rates %	1981 9.2	1984 12.1	1985 12.4	1987 11.6

Average Earnings	1981	1984	1985	1986
Male	130.7	161.9	175.0	188.9
Female	90.8	109.7	124.3	136.9

Housing Completions	1981 2,096*	1984 2,979	1985 2,821	1986 2,103[†]

Industrial Floorspace ('000 sq. metres)	1981 1,040.4	1984 1,061.3	1985 1,058.8

Employment			
Industrial Establishments	1987 = 1,582		
Employees %	–100	100+	1,000+
	69.8	6.3	0.2

Rateable Value 1985 £m.	Total 103.516	Domestic % 63.0	Commercial % 21.1	Industrial % 4.4	Other % 11.6

Local Authority Expenditure (£'000)	83/84 224,928	84/85 228,439	86/87 258,092e

Economic Development Cost per capita (£)	82/83	84/85	85/86
	0.30	0.18	0.18e

* Total of district figures

[†] Only 9 months' figures available for 1986

e Estimate

For notes on statistics see p. xi

Covering an area of 179,513 hectares, the county is largely rural with large areas of outstanding beauty, such as the South Downs and the Weald. It is also an important tourist area, with the holiday resorts of Brighton, Eastbourne and Hastings along its coastline.

Industry and Employment

By far the majority of East Sussex employment is in the service sector: 71 per cent of jobs are service jobs, compared to 61 per cent nationally. On the other side of the coin, the size of the county's manufacturing sector is very small, 16 per cent of all employment compared to 27 per cent nationally. The biggest employers in East Sussex are mostly located in Brighton, Hove and Lewes and they are also almost exclusively service sector businesses – finance, professional services, public utilities, health, education and public administration. The hotel and catering sector accounts for 5 per cent of East Sussex employment, but it is estimated that, altogether, 7–8 per cent of the county's jobs (about 17,000) are dependent on the tourist and conference trade.

The great majority of the county's larger manufacturing companies have, over the past decade, either contracted in employment terms, or closed their local plants completely. Between 1971 and 1981 over 5,500 manufacturing jobs were lost in the county, most of them due to closures and staff reductions in engineering firms in Brighton and Hove. Although the traditional heavy manufacturing industries hit hardest by the recession are under-represented in the county, the light engineering and machine tool producers which represent a large proportion of the East Sussex manufacturing sector have suffered the 'knock-on' effects of a contracting domestic market for means of production.

The great 'shake out' of labour that has occurred in manufacturing, together with the application of new labour-saving technology which is being undertaken to meet competition and achieve new orders, means that, even when the current recession eases, existing manufacturing firms are unlikely to expand their workforces significantly. Any significant increase in the number of manufacturing jobs is likely to depend on product innovation and associated new product enterprises, yet there is little evidence in East Sussex of the 'new wave', 'high tech' research and manufacturing concerns. East Sussex has by far the lowest proportion of 'high tech' employment out of all the counties in the South East. Only the Isle of Wight has fewer 'high tech' jobs than East Sussex.

The Structure Plan aims to develop light industries in the county and to generate growth in the economically less buoyant areas of the county, particularly Hastings, where income levels are low and where the tourist industry has suffered a decline.

The estimated economically active population in 1985 was 278,430, a rise of 4,800 on the 1981 figure. Unemployment, however, has remained relatively stable throughout the 1980s. In December 1982 the rate was 12 per cent and in February 1987 it was 11.6 per cent, representing 28,940 people.

East Sussex

Local Authority Initiatives

County Council activity has been largely limited to providing information on the local economy and developing some sites. A Rural Development Area (RDA) has been designated around Rye.

See: *The East Sussex Economy: Employment Review*, published by Planning Department, 1985.

Contact: Planning Department, Southover House, Southover Road, Lewes, BN7 17A.

ESSEX

Total Population ('000)	1981	1984	1985
	1,483.0	1,496.7	1,504.7

Main Districts			
Basildon	153.2	156.6	156.3
Braintree	112.7	114.7	115.6
Chelmsford	139.6	146.1	147.9
Colchester	138.2	140.7	143.1
Epping Forest	117.0	114.8	114.7
Southend-on-Sea	157.6	157.4	158.2
Tendring	114.7	118.9	121.2
Thurrock	127.4	124.4	124.4

Age Structure 1985 ('000)	0–4	5–14	15–29	30–44	45–59/64	60/65–74	75+
	94.4	197.6	337.9	314.7	290.0	175.2	94.9

Unemployment Rates %	1981	1984	1985	1987
	9.2	12.7	12.8	11.2

Average Earnings	1981	1984	1985	1986
Male	143.5	182.5	197.3	209.2
Female	90.9	116.8	122.4	133.7

Housing Completions	1981	1984	1985	1986
	5,932*	6,219*	5,335*	5,366*†

Industrial Floorspace ('000 sq. metres)	1981	1984	1985
	4,696.0	4,961.0	4,868.9

Employment			
Industrial Establishments	1987 = 2,961		
Employees %	–100	100+	1,000+
	79.3	8.0	0.8

Rateable Value 1985 £m.	Total	Domestic %	Commercial %	Industrial %	Other %
	244.630	57.9	19.7	9.5	12.9

Local Authority Expenditure (£'000)	83/84	84/85	86/87
	539,143	527,477	610,742e

Economic Development Cost per capita (£)	82/83	84/85	85/86
	0.13	0.45	0.26e

* Total of district figures
† Only 9 months' figures available for 1986
e Estimate
For notes on statistics see p. xi

Essex

Essex covers an area of 367,192 hectares; activity in the county is a mixture of agriculture, fishing, industry and tourism. The ports of Tilbury, Parkeston and Harwich deal with continental traffic, along with Stansted airport. Agricultural activities include cereal, fruit growing and market gardening, and various industries are situated particularly in the towns along the Thames. There are a number of resorts and country parks, with Southend being the largest.

Industry and Employment

A large number of Essex residents commute to offices in London for work. This has led to an above-average proportion of manufacturing jobs in the county, with electrical and mechanical engineering being particularly important. The above-average number of people in manufacturing has also produced higher unemployment levels than in the rest of the South East.

The Structure Plan was adopted in 1982 and has yet to be revised. The plan noted that large scale housing and population growth had exceeded employment growth and that the balance must be redressed. The plan envisages that the ratio of jobs to workers will be increased over the plan period. So, although the housing policy was restrictive, the county believed that the resident working population was numerically sufficient for the needs of employers even after their expansionary employment policy was implemented. The plan also stresses that most new jobs are expected to come from the expansion of existing firms and the population will continue to grow, although at a lower rate than in recent years. OPCS forecast a rise of 5.1 per cent between 1985 and 1995, although Cambridge Econometrics forecast a higher rise, of 8.3 per cent . The main area of growth is in South Essex and the Structure Plan also identifies the lack of employment opportunities in Tendring district.

Unemployment at February 1987 was 11.2 per cent, representing 59,858 people.

Local Authority Initiatives

Mainly promotional activities by the County Council.

See: *Economic Growth and Planning Policies in the South East*, published by the Housing Research Foundation, November 1986.

Contact: Planning Department, Globe House, New Street, Chelmsford, CM1 1LF.

New Towns

Basildon was designated in 1949. Original population: 25,000; present population (31 July 1986): 104,600. The Development Corporation was wound up in 1986 and its final report noted that 42,530 were employed in the town and factory space completed covered 856,814 square metres. The housing stock stood at 29,363 dwellings. Although new jobs have been created the town still has an unemployment rate higher than the South East region generally.

Harlow was designated in 1947. Original population: 4,500; present population (31 March 1984): 78,000. The Development Corporation was dissolved in 1980. Employment in 1984 was 44,700 and 233 factories had been completed, covering 517,340 square metres of floorspace. In 1984, unemployment was still relatively low, at 7.9 per cent.

South Woodham Ferres is a private new town, established in 1975 and covering 526 hectares. It is described as a freestanding new 'country' town with a current population of 13,700. Planned population is 17,500.

In February 1987 the plan by Consortium Developments, a group of nine large housebuilders, to build a new town of 5,100 houses at *Tillingham Hall* was rejected by the Environment Secretary. This was based on the view that there was no shortage of housing land in Essex, or the South East generally.

GLOUCESTERSHIRE

Total Population ('000)			1981	1984	1985	
			505.7	509.2	511.4	

Main Districts						
Cheltenham			86.1	86.3	86.0	
Forest of Dean			73.2	73.5	74.1	
Gloucester			92.6	91.6	91.1	
Stroud			102.2	103.6	104.5	
Tewkesbury			81.8	83.3	84.1	

Age Structure 1985 ('000)	0–4	5–14	15–29	30–44	45–59/64	60/65–74	75+
	30.8	64.7	116.7	102.6	99.2	62.6	34.8

Unemployment Rates %	1981	1984	1985	1987
	7.5	10.1	10.4	8.9

Average Earnings	1981	1984	1985	1986
Male	136.9	168.2	182.7	197.6
Female	89.1	109.0	118.0	126.1

Housing Completions	1981	1984	1985	1986
	2,015	2,253	2,752	2,148[†]

Industrial Floorspace ('000 sq. metres)	1981	1984	1985
	2,785.0	2,851.1	2,847.2

Employment			
Industrial Establishments	1987 = 1,777		
Employees %	–100	100+	1,000+
	69.3	8.0	0.5

Rateable Value 1985 £m.	Total	Domestic %	Commercial %	Industrial %	Other %
	68.130	54.6	19.7	11.1	14.7

Local Authority Expenditure (£'000)	83/84	84/85	86/87
	190,029	185,391	209,784e

Economic Development Cost per capita (£)	82/83	84/85	85/86
	0.22	0.20	0.18e

[†] Only 9 months' figures available for 1986

e Estimate

For notes on statistics see p. xi

The county covers an area of 264,258 hectares and recent years have seen a diversification in the area's economy. This is reflected in the growth of the service sector and the development of new industries to replace the older industries, such as mining and wool. It is a historic county with significant areas of natural beauty, including the Forest of Dean and the Cotswolds.

Industry and Employment

In the early 1970s the county experienced particularly rapid employment growth, well above the national rate. This was primarily due to the 'office boom' in the county when a number of large office establishments located within the main centres, notably Gloucester and Cheltenham, and this growth is now reflected in the present employment structure of the county – services account for just over 60 per cent of employment. Tourism is important within the service economy: it accounts for 10,000 jobs and sustains an annual expenditure of £74 million in the county. Agriculture is also a big employer and various other industries are developing, particularly along the M5 corridor.

The 'office boom' was accompanied by steady population growth. Between 1971 and 1981 the population grew by 6.2 per cent, and a further increase of 1.1 per cent has occurred between 1981 and 1985.

Unemployment is well below the South West average although some of the rural areas, particularly in the Forest of Dean, have much higher rates. At February 1987, the unemployment rate was 8.9 per cent, representing 19,723 people.

Local Authority Initiatives

The County Council's Economic Development Sub-Committee has produced a new 'Programme for Action' and key themes include better access to financial advice for local companies, a training strategy, aiding the competitiveness and faster growth of local companies, and measures to help the unemployed. Sites, start up finance and inward investment are also covered. Part of the Forest of Dean is a Rural Development Area.

See: *Economic Development Strategy – Programme for Action*, published by Planning Department, September 1986.

Contact: Employment Promotion Department, Shire Hall, Gloucester, GL1 2TN.

GREATER LONDON

Total Population ('000)	1981	1984	1985
	6,805.7	6,756.0	6,767.5

London Boroughs			
City of London	5.4	5.4	5.1
Barking and Dagenham	151.6	149.4	148.6
Barnet	295.2	298.2	301.2
Bexley	217.1	218.4	218.5
Brent	254.2	254.9	254.9
Bromley	298.5	298.4	297.9
Camden	179.1	177.3	180.4
Croydon	321.1	318.9	319.0
Ealing	282.2	288.7	292.4
Enfield	261.1	263.3	265.0
Greenwich	215.6	216.0	216.2
Hackney	185.1	187.9	187.5
Hammersmith & Fulham	151.3	150.7	150.9
Haringey	207.2	200.1	197.2
Harrow	199.0	201.4	201.7
Havering	242.2	239.7	238.5
Hillingdon	233.3	232.2	232.3
Hounslow	203.9	197.8	195.6
Islington	166.1	165.2	167.9
Kensington and Chelsea	140.1	136.0	137.6
Kingston upon Thames	134.3	134.1	133.9
Lambeth	253.0	244.2	243.5
Lewisham	236.4	232.1	232.4
Merton	167.6	164.0	164.5
Newham	212.8	209.4	208.6
Redbridge	229.2	226.5	228.0
Richmond upon Thames	161.8	160.6	161.5
Southwark	218.3	215.6	215.9
Sutton	170.1	169.6	169.6
Tower Hamlets	145.2	144.6	147.1
Waltham Forest	217.5	215.1	216.2
Wandsworth	262.0	258.3	258.8
Westminster, City of	188.2	182.0	179.1

Age Structure 1985 ('000)	0–4	5–14	15–29	30–44	45–59/64	60/65–74	75+
	438.1	776.0	1,664.9	1,410.4	1,265.3	764.8	448.0

Unemployment Rates %	1981	1984	1985	1987
	6.7	10.0	10.2	10.0

Average Earnings	1981	1984	1985	1986
Male	163.8	214.7	233.2	255.0
Female	107.4	142.8	154.4	169.3

Housing Completions	1981	1984	1985	1986
	–	10,498	8,707	6,768†

Industrial Floorspace		*1981*	*1984*	*1985*		
('000 sq. metres)		22,495.2	20,866.3	20,452.2		
Employment						
ındustrial Establishments		1987 = 20,132				
Employees %		−100	100+	1,000+		
		74.4	6.6	0.3		
Rateable Value 1985	*Total*	*Domestic %*	*Commercial %*	*Industrial %*	*Other %*	
£m.	−	−	−	−	−	
Local Authority Expenditure		*83/84*	*84/85*	*86/87*		
(£'000)		−	−	−		
Economic Development Cost		*82/83*	*84/85*	*85/86*		
per capita (£)						
		0.71	3.02#	1.88#		

− Figures not available

† Only 9 months' figures for 1986

Average of economic development costs of all London Boroughs

For notes on statistics see p. xi

Greater London covers an area of 157,994 hectares and within this area live over 6.5 million people. London is the nation's capital and houses the country's government and central administration. Up until April 1986 the Greater London Council (GLC) administered the area but this has now been abolished. The London Residuary Body (LRB) has taken over some of the functions of the GLC and this in turn will be wound up in 1991. Greater London now has nineteen outer London boroughs and three inner London boroughs, plus the City of London.

Many companies have their head offices within the Greater London boundary, but the area also has a wide diversity of manufacturing industry including food and drink (particularly brewing), instrument engineering, electrical and electronic engineering, clothing, furniture and printing. Heathrow and Gatwick are international airports nearby and various road and rail networks converge on the area.

Industry and Employment

In June 1978 employment in Greater London was 3,679,000 but by December 1985 it had fallen to 3,545,000. In all, London lost 381,000 jobs and gained 246,000, making a net loss of 135,000 (3.7 per cent) over the period. Of the jobs lost, 50 per cent were in manufacturing, 20 per cent in education, health and other services, 18 per cent in transport and communications, 8 per cent in construction and 3 per cent in energy and water industries. Of the jobs gained, 64 per cent were in financial services, 19 per cent in distribution, hotels and catering and 17 per cent in central and local government services. The general structure of employment in the area is as follows:

The increase in employment in services is evident in the capital, where expansion in financial and business services has been particularly noticeable. London is one of the world's centres of banking, insurance and financial services, and London and

Greater London

1980 SIC	June 78 ('000)	Dec. 85 ('000)	Diff. ('000)	%
0 Agr., For., Fish	1.8	2	+.2	+11
1 Energy & Water	55.2	44	−11.2	−20
2 Met./Chem. Mfr	78.0	62	−16.0	−21
3 Met. Eng. & Vehic.	347.6	253	−94.6	−27
4 Other Mfr	339.8	258	−81.8	−24
2+3+4 Mfr Total	765.4	573	−192.4	−25
5 Construction	175.5	144	−31.5	−18
6 Dist. Hotel & Cat.	697.4	743	+45.6	+7
7 Trans. & Comm's	392.5	324	−68.5	−18
8 Bank, Ins. & Finance	495.2	653	+157.8	+32
91–2 Pub. Ad. & Def.	335.0	377	+42.0	+13
93–9 Ed. Hea. & Other	761.6	684	−77.6	−10
0–9 TOTAL	3,679.8	3,545	−134.8	−4

the surrounding counties account for 2/3 of UK advertising and market research companies, over half of the UK research establishments, half of the UK central government offices, and nearly half of non-food wholesale distribution in England. Given high rents and government incentives, however, there has been some decentralization of offices outside the capital in recent years. London is also important as a tourist centre and 2/3 of income from overseas tourists is generated in London.

A quarter of the new jobs in London since 1978 are women's part-time jobs and there has been an increase in commuting which is likely to continue. Between 1971 and 1981 net in-commuting was increasing by about 8,500 people per year and it is estimated that, since 1978, 60,000 jobs have been taken by people outside London. The number of economically active people in London has also been falling, with a drop of 10 per cent between 1971 and 1981. GLC projections in 1985 suggest that the number of economically active will remain fairly constant throughout the 1980s, with a rise in London's workforce of only 65,000 between 1984 and 2001.

The revised *Greater London Development Plans (GDLP)* produced before abolition were based on the assumption that the population of the area would decline. Labour shortages would be largely mitigated by in-commuting but dwelling space would be increased – 203,000 new dwellings proposed between 1983 and 1992. The plans also suggested that London's physical resources are going to waste. Over 35 square miles of land is currently unused, 3.3 million square metres of factory space is vacant and more than 1.6 million square metres of office space is immediately available for letting. Therefore the plans placed more weight on meeting the wide range of community needs and less on meeting the market demand for offices.

Unemployment at February 1987 was 10 per cent, representing 390,684 people.

Local Authority Initiatives

Before abolition, the GLC was involved in a wide range of activities, including a sector-by-sector development of a London Industrial Strategy, development of the London Labour Plan, establishment of the Greater London Enterprise Board, support for co-ops and new business types, policies for disadvantaged groups, setting up Contract Compliance/Equal Opportunities Units etc. Most boroughs now have some economic strategy, ranging from Wandsworth with policies aimed particularly at developing the private sector, to Southwark, Islington, Camden, where policies emphasize the job generation role of local authorities.

See: *A City Divided – London's Economy since 1979*, published by London Strategic Policy Unit (LSPU), 1986.

Contact: LSPU, Middlesex House, 20 Vauxhall Bridge Road, London, SW1V 2SB.

Enterprise Zone

Designated on 26 April 1982 in the Isle of Dogs, it covers 147 hectares of land, and at December 1985 had 256 establishments, employing 2,700 people.

Science Parks

The South Bank Technopark, sponsored by South Bank Technopark Limited and Prudential Assurance, was established in April 1985. It covers 1.7 acres and at December 1986 had 36 companies on site.

Brunel University Science Park was established in June 1986. It covers 6.4 acres and, at December 1986, had eight companies on site.

GREATER MANCHESTER

Total Population ('000)	1981	1984	1985
	2,619.2	2,588.3	2,582.6

Main Districts			
Bolton	262.3	261.3	261.2
Bury	176.7	173.8	173.3
Manchester	462.6	454.7	451.1
Oldham	221.4	220.4	219.7
Rochdale	208.2	206.2	206.1
Salford	247.0	242.5	240.0
Stockport	290.5	289.1	291.2
Tameside	218.5	215.3	215.5
Trafford	221.7	217.7	217.8
Wigan	310.3	307.3	306.7

Age Structure 1985 ('000)	0–4	5–14	15–29	30–44	45–59/64	60/65–74	75+
	172.0	340.0	619.8	513.6	482.4	297.0	157.8

Unemployment Rates (%)	1981	1984	1985	1987
	11.2	14.7	15.5	14.6

Average Earnings	1981	1984	1985	1986
Male	136.6	171.5	183.5	198.6
Female	88.2	110.9	119.6	130.6

Housing Completions	1981	1984	1985	1986
	7,944*	7,175	5,618	4,259*†

Industrial Floorspace ('000 sq. metres)	1981	1984	1985
	22,924.0	20,986.6	20,265.6

Employment			
Industrial Establishments	1987 = 5,879		
Employees %	–100	100+	1,000+
	75.1	10.9	0.7

Rateable Value 1985 £m.	Total	Domestic %	Commercial %	Industrial %	Other %
	338.500	50.7	23.9	11.1	14.4

Local Authority Expenditure (£'000)	83/84	84/85	86/87
	405,379	345,118	x

Economic Development Cost per Capita (£)	82/83	84/85	85/86
	0.69	1.13	1.26e

* Total of district figures
† Only 9 months' figures for 1986
x Figures not provided
e Estimate
For notes on statistics see p. xi

One of the largest urban areas in the country, Greater Manchester covers 728,674 hectares and has a population of 2.5 million. Up to April 1986 the area was locally governed by the Greater Manchester Council, but this has now been abolished and replaced with a residuary body. There are ten district authorities in the area, all but one having populations of over 200,000. Coalmining and textiles are the established industries but in recent years industries such as light engineering, transport, and warehousing have become important. It is also the second largest financial centre in the country and international communications points include Manchester Airport and the Port of Manchester.

Industry and Employment

By the early 1980s 1,031,000 people were employed in the area, with 296,000 of those in Manchester itself and 735,000 in the other districts. This represents a 10.4 per cent fall on the total 1971 figure of 1,151,000. Structural changes have also seen a fall in the size of the manufacturing sector and a rise in services:

	Manufacturing %	Construction %	Services %
1971	41.4	4.3	54.3
1978	35.1	4.5	60.4
1981	30.4	5.0	64.6

The fall in manufacturing's share is even more pronounced in Manchester itself: by the early 1980s it accounted for only 21.8 per cent of employees in employment, with services at 73.8 per cent. In the nine boroughs outside Manchester manufacturing accounted for 38.7 per cent of employment.

Population is also declining – between 1979 and 1985 Greater Manchester lost 4.2 per cent of its population. Manchester's population declined by 6 per cent in the same period, with a 2.4 per cent decline in other districts. Within an overall decline the most notable changes are that the number of children below school age (0–4) has fallen dramatically, the number of young people (16–34) has risen and the number of people over 75 has risen considerably.

Unemployment at February 1987 was 14.6 per cent, representing 172,756 people.

Local Authority Initiatives

The Greater Manchester Economic Development Corporation set up by the County Council still exists with the support of the private sector and the district councils, although its funding beyond the late 1980s is in doubt. Manchester City Council has an Economic Development Department which has recently produced an employment plan, centred around direct job creation by the Council and the multiplier effect on the local economy. A training strategy is a part of the plan.

Greater Manchester

Other authorities developing strategies include Bury, Oldham and Rochdale, which has developed a local purchasing strategy.

See: *A Strategy for Employment*, published by Manchester City Council, February 1987.

Contact: Greater Manchester Economic Development Corporation, Bernard House, Piccadilly Gardens, Manchester, M1 4DD.

Enterprise Zone

Two sites, in Salford and Trafford, were established in August 1981. The zone covers 352 hectares and in 1985 had 257 establishments, employing 4,200 people.

Science Parks

Manchester Science Park was established in December 1984 and sponsors are the City Council, Ciba Geigy, Ferranti, Fothergill and Harvey and Granada TV. It covers 15.5 acres and by December 1986 there were eleven companies on site.

Bolton Technology Centre was established in April 1986, involving English Estates, Bolton Council and the Institute of Technology. It covers 2.5 acres and had ten companies at December 1986.

Salford University Business Park, involving Salford City Council, Salford University and English Estates, will be established in 1988.

HAMPSHIRE

Total Population ('000)		1981 1,488.5	1984 1,509.2	1985 1,523.9

Main Districts

	1981	1984	1985
Basingstoke and Deane	131.0	136.3	137.6
Havant	115.7	117.4	118.5
New Forest	145.5	151.8	155.6
Portsmouth	191.4	188.6	187.9
Southampton	209.9	203.9	202.3

Age Structure 1985 ('000)	0–4 97.0	5–14 195.5	15–29 383.6	30–44 311.5	45–59/64 278.6	60/65–74 164.9	75+ 92.8

Unemployment Rates %	1981 7.7	1984 9.9	1985 10.3	1987 9.8

Average Earnings	1981	1984	1985	1986
Male	140.3	181.1	196.4	212.0
Female	89.5	116.8	126.2	134.7

Housing Completions	1981 7,398*	1984 8,960	1985 8,855	1986 5,784*†

Industrial Floorspace ('000 sq. metres)	1981 4,196.5	1984 4,217.3	1985 4,245.3

Employment

Industrial Establishments	1987 = 3,959		
Employees %	–100	100+	1,000+
	77.9	7.7	0.6

Rateable Value 1985 £m.	Total 222.042	Domestic % 54.0	Commercial % 20.4	Industrial % 10.1	Other % 15.5

Local Authority Expenditure (£'000)	83/84 561,051	84/85 540,850	86/87 600,736e

Economic Development Cost per capita (£)	82/83 0.37	84/85 0.28	85/86 0.21e

* Total of district figures
† Only 9 months' figures for 1986
e Estimate
For notes on statistics see p. xi

Hampshire covers 377,358 hectares and is the largest non-metropolitan county in England, with a population of just over 1.5 million. The major settlements and most of the industrial developments are around Portsmouth and Southampton, which are also key commercial deep sea and ferry ports. Electronics are the newer industries, alongside engineering and Royal Navy sites. Agriculture is also important, although most people are employed in services. There are areas of natural beauty, particularly around the New Forest.

Industry and Employment

Despite many fluctuations of the national economy the county has gained a steadily increasing share of national employment. In 1961 the county had less than 22 out of every 1,000 jobs nationally but in 1981 this had risen to 28. Most people are employed in services/construction, representing 69.4 per cent of total employment, followed by manufacturing at 27.2 per cent and others at 3.4 per cent. Engineering accounts for over 60 per cent of manufacturing employment although there have been job losses in this sector in recent years – electrical and mechanical engineering are leading sectors followed by marine engineering. The largest individual employer is the Royal Navy, directly employing 25,000, although 6,000 jobs have been lost with the rundown of the Royal Dockyard, Portsmouth.

High technology is becoming increasingly important. It now accounts for approximately 10 per cent of Hampshire's total workforce, and a recent Council survey identified 46,400 jobs in this sector. Employment in this sector is concentrated in the large firms and the average size of electronic firms in the county is greater than the national or regional average.

Hampshire is covered by four Structure Plans. South Hampshire, which includes Southampton and Portsmouth, is seen as the 'growth area' and in the other areas there are limits on growth. In the south west conservation and environmental protection are considered paramount. In mid-Hampshire employment growth is restricted in order to limit any consequential housing demand, on the assumption that new housing demand is due to people drawn to the area by new jobs. Economic growth, however, is encouraged around Andover. In north east Hampshire a similar approach has been adopted, with new office and industrial development concentrated around Basingstoke, and to a lesser extent Farnborough.

Unemployment at February 1987 was 9.8 per cent, representing 60,934 people.

Local Authority Initiatives

Apart from traditional policies of site provision the Council provides support for small firms and start-ups, is active in training provision and in marketing and has established the Hampshire Development Association, with some district councils. It has also initiated a £3m urban regeneration programme in Portsmouth and Southampton.

See: *Hampshire County Council's Support for the Economy*, published by the Planning Unit, February 1986.

Contact: County Planning Officer, The Castle, Winchester, SO23 8UJ.

Science Park

The Chilworth Centre for Technology has recently been established involving the County Council, Southampton City Council, Test Valley Borough Council and Southampton University.

Freeport

The first UK freeport, opened in April 1984, is based in Southampton docks. Its principal function is warehousing and it appears to be doing better than the other six sites in the UK.

HEREFORD AND WORCESTER

Total Population ('000)			1981 636.4	1984 645.3	1985 650.8	

Main Districts	1981	1984	1985
Bromsgrove	88.2	88.7	89.4
Malvern Hills	85.2	85.8	85.7
Worcester	75.9	76.2	76.2
Wychavon	95.4	97.2	98.1
Wyre Forest	91.7	93.0	93.1

Age Structure 1985 ('000)	0–4 40.5	5–14 87.5	15–29 146.9	30–44 138.6	45–59/64 124.8	60/65–74 73.9	75+ 38.6

Unemployment Rates %	1981 10.1	1984 13.7	1985 14.3	1987 13.0

Average Earnings	1981	1984	1985	1986
Male	124.6	158.6	176.1	184.2
Female	87.3	110.4	116.4	126.3

Housing Completions	1981 2,747*	1984 3,021*	1985 3,178	1986 1,949†

Industrial Floorspace ('000 sq. metres)	1981 3,306.8	1984 3,324.9	1985 3,315.8

Employment			
Industrial Establishments	1987 = 2,623		
Employees %	–100 78.9	100+ 5.5	1,000+ 0.4

Rateable Value 1985 £m	Total 90.446	Domestic % 58.2	Commercial % 17.8	Industrial % 10.8	Other % 13.2

Local Authority Expenditure (£'000)	83/84 230,783	84/85 237,267	86/87 263,204e

Economic Development Cost per capita (£)	82/83 0.03	84/85 −0.02	85/86 0.04e

* Total of district figures
† Only 9 months' figures for 1986
e Estimate
For notes on statistics see p. xi

A county covering 392,678 hectares, Hereford and Worcester is situated between the outskirts of Birmingham and the Welsh border. It is essentially a rural county, including the Wye Valley, the Vale of Evesham, a section of the Cotswolds, the Malvern Hills and the Black Mountains. Industrial development is concentrated around Hereford, Worcester, Droitwich and Redditch New Town. The agricultural and horticultural industries are major sectors but industry, particularly engineering, is represented notably around Worcester.

Industry and Employment

The population of the area has been gradually rising – between 1971 and 1981 the population rose by 12.9 per cent from 552,945 to 624,393, and a further rise of 2.2 per cent occurred between 1981 and 1985. Future population growth will be concentrated around Hereford, Leominster and Ross-on-Wye. Industrial development is also being encouraged in these towns as well as in the main urban centres in the north east of the county – areas such as Kidderminster, Bromsgrove, Stourport, Bewdley, Worcester and Redditch New Town. Engineering, textiles, and food and drink manufacturing are the principal manufacturing sectors, although over 60 per cent of those employed are in services. There is no one regional service centre and most jobs are split between the two cathedral cities of Hereford and Worcester.

The latest County Structure Plan was approved in 1985, but in Redditch and Bromsgrove there are problems with green belt areas. The Councils have designated all land outside the towns as green belt, but the Secretary of State has told the Councils to take land from the green belt for potential development in the 1990s.

Unemployment at February 1987 was 13 per cent, representing 30,906 people.

Local Authority Initiatives

Mainly the provision of serviced sites and premises and loan schemes for small businesses. The west of the county is a Rural Development Area.

See: *Hereford and Worcester County Structure Plan: Approved Written Statement*, published by Planning Department.

Contact: Economic Development Officer, County Offices, Bath Street, Hereford, HR1 2HQ.

New Town

Redditch was designated in 1964. Original population: 32,000; present population (31 March 1985): 73,500. In 1985, there were 487,368 square metres of industrial floorspace.

HERTFORDSHIRE

Total Population ('000)	1981 964.8	1984 980.3	1985 986.1

Main Districts			
Dacorum	130.8	132.4	133.1
East Hertfordshire	109.4	115.0	116.9
North Hertfordshire	108.0	110.6	111.4
St Albans	125.3	127.7	128.8
Welwyn Hatfield	94.1	94.0	94.0

Age Structure 1985 ('000)	0–4 61.6	5–14 128.4	15–29 227.8	30–44 208.3	45–59/64 199.5	60/65–74 107.0	75+ 53.5

Unemployment Rates %	1981 5.5	1984 7.8	1985 7.5	1987 6.8

Average Earnings	1981	1984	1985	1986
Male	147.8	188.2	203.7	223.0
Female	95.1	117.0	131.6	145.3

Housing Completions	1981 3,171*	1984 5,029	1985 4,103	1986 2,479*†

Industrial Floorspace ('000 sq. metres)	1981 4,147.8	1984 4,028.0	1985 3,912.5

Employment Industrial Establishments	1987 = 2,930		
Employees %	–100 61.4	100+ 8.2	1,000+ 0.6

Rateable Value 1985 £m.	Total 176.634	Domestic % 53.4	Commercial % 22.4	Industrial % 12.0	Other % 12.2

Local Authority Expenditure (£'000)	83/84 368,094	84/85 x	86/87 406,059e

Economic Development Cost per capita (£)	82/83 –	84/85 0.17	85/86 0.17e

* Total of district figures
† Only 9 months' figures for 1986
x Figures not provided
e Estimate
– Figures not available
For notes on statistics see p. xi

Hertfordshire covers 163,418 hectares to the north of London. It lies at the centre of the main traffic routes from London to the Midlands and the North and has traditionally been a centre for the printing industry. Newer industries in the area include computers and electronics, plastics and pharmaceuticals.

Industry and Employment

The location of the county near London, its good communications network, and a variety of industrial locations based largely around a group of postwar new or newly developing towns, such as Stevenage, Welwyn Garden City, Hemel Hempstead and Hatfield, have, until recently, helped the area to ride the recession relatively well. The unemployment rate is the fourth lowest in the country, at around 7 per cent, and the central triangle of the county around St Albans, Welwyn Garden City and Potters Bar has been least affected by the recession. The north of the county is experiencing heavier job losses; Letchworth and Stevenage have been particularly hit by closures at major companies.

The revised Structure Plan, altered in 1984, eased restrictions on industrial development in the county and noted that more accommodation for office employment would be needed. Cambridge Econometrics forecast an employment growth of 4.6 per cent between 1985 and 1995 and the revised Structure Plan anticipates 52,500 new dwellings between 1981 and 1996.

Unemployment at February 1987 was 6.8 per cent, representing 28,248 people.

Local Authority Initiatives

Mainly site/estate developments.

See: *Economic Growth and Planning Policies in the South East*, published by the Housing Research Foundation, November 1986.

Contact: Planning, County Hall, Hertford, SG13 8DN.

New Towns

Hatfield was designated in 1948. Original population: 8,500; present population (31 March 1984): 25,200. The Development Corporation was dissolved in 1966. The main employment comes from Hawker Siddeley and British Aerospace, although a number of new industries are now represented. At March 1984, 24,100 were employed in the town and the main industrial area, and unemployment was 7.9 per cent.

Hemel Hempstead was designated in 1947. Original population: 21,000; present population (31 March 1984): 78,000. The Development Corporation was dissolved in 1962. 45,900 were employed in the town and main industrial area at March 1984 and the unemployment rate was 9 per cent. Industrial floorspace was 488,060 square metres.

Stevenage was designated in 1946. Original population: 6,700; present population (31 March 1984): 73,600. The Development Corporation was dissolved in 1966. Employment at March 1984 was 52,600 and, after extensive closures in

Hertfordshire

1980/82, unemployment was 7.9 per cent by 1984. Manufacturing floorspace covered 520,100 square metres.

Welwyn Garden City was designated in 1948. Original population: 18,500; present population (31 March 1984): 41,800. The Development Corporation was dissolved in 1966. Britain's prototype new town had, until recently, the lowest new town unemployment rate at 5.4 per cent (1982). It has now risen to 7.9 per cent (1984), with 47,400 employed.

HUMBERSIDE

Total Population ('000)		1981 857.6	1984 851.6	1985 850.0	

Main Districts					
Beverley		107.0	108.0	108.3	
Cleethorpes		68.6	68.5	68.8	
Great Grimsby		92.7	91.7	90.9	
Kingston upon Hull		273.7	265.6	262.0	
East Yorkshire		75.3	77.2	78.3	

Age Structure 1985 ('000)	0–4 54.5	5–14 113.6	15–29 196.7	30–44 166.8	45–59/64 165.9	60/65–74 99.7	75+ 52.8

Unemployment Rates %	1981 12.7	1984 16.1	1985 17.5	1987 16.8

Average Earnings	1981	1984	1985	1986
Male	132.4	165.7	181.8	192.6
Female	83.1	104.7	115.9	123.6

Housing Completions	1981 3,419*	1984 2,898	1985 3,180	1986 1,722*†

Industrial Floorspace ('000 sq. metres)	1981 4,827.0	1984 4,726.3	1985 4,627.9

Employment				
Industrial Establishments	1987 = 858			
Employees %		–100 73.7	100+ 11.0	1,000+ 0.9

Rateable Value 1985 £m.	Total 101.295	Domestic % 48.5	Commercial % 18.8	Industrial % 16.6	Other % 16.1

Local Authority Expenditure (£'000)	83/84 372,245	84/85 372,149	86/87 417,642e

Economic Development Cost per capita (£)	82/83 0.17	84/85 0.30	85/86 0.65e

* Total of district figures
† Only 9 months' figures for 1986
e Estimate
For notes on statistics see p. xi

Humberside

The county covers 351,204 hectares, most of which (85 per cent) is in agricultural use. The main industries are food and drink, chemicals, steel, agriculture and fishing, transport and distribution. Major towns are Hull and Grimsby which, along with Immingham and Goole, are important sea ports handling approximately 29 million tonnes of cargo a year and 490,000 passengers. North Sea oil and gas resources are nearby and the Humber is one of the few deep water estuaries in Britain which has potential for large scale development. Humberside Airport offers national flights and flights to Europe.

Industry and Employment

The recent performance of sectors important to the county can be summarized as follows: primary sector remains important despite job losses; manufacturing accounts for one third of jobs, similar to the national average, and three sectors predominate – steel, food and drink and chemicals; construction accounts for some 7 per cent of the county's employment; the transport and distribution service industries represent the second largest employing sector despite job losses; the service sector is the biggest employer although private services are under-represented. The county's tourist-related jobs fall in this sector.

Humberside is among the most disadvantaged areas in Europe – 38th out of 149 regions in an EEC league table with the worst area at the top. Not all, however, is gloomy. The industrial structure is broadly based and there are good links with Europe – Hull and Immingham are the 9th and 10th largest UK ports respectively, dealing with 3.1 per cent and 2.6 per cent of UK visible trade. A wide range of financial aid is available and planning applications for all kinds of development are back to their previous peak of the late 1970s. There is a boom in retailing investment throughout the county worth some £70 million.

Unemployment at November 1986 was 16.6 per cent, covering 56,978 people, due mainly to losses in fishing, steel, and port-related activities. The gap between numbers of people wanting to work and jobs available has widened considerably since 1979. Over the next five years more than 15,000 people could join the workforce and around 3,000 new jobs a year are needed just to prevent further rises in unemployment.

Local Authority Initiatives

The Economic Development Unit (EDU) has produced a new economic strategy concentrating on stimulating investment and jobs from within Humberside, attracting inward investment, developing training initiatives to maximize the skills of the workforce, obtaining maximum aid particularly from the EEC and providing a corporate research and information service.

See: *Helping Humberside Work – A Strategy and Programme for Economic Development*, published by the EDU, April 1986.

Contact: J. Siddall, Economic Development Officer, County Hall, Beverley, HU17 9BA.

Enterprise Zones

Two zones are based in the area: *Scunthorpe*, designated in September 1983, and *Glanford*, designated in April 1984. Twenty-five firms are on both sites, employing 800 people (1985).

Science Park

The Newlands Centre was established in Hull in December 1984, a venture involving the University, the City Council and English Estates. At the end of 1986, twelve companies were on the site of three acres.

ISLE OF WIGHT

Total Population			1981	1984		1985	
('000)			118.1	120.9		122.9	

Main Districts							
Medina			67.9	68.7		69.7	
South Wight			50.2	52.2		53.2	

Age Structure 1985	0–4	5–14	15–29	30–44	45–59/64	60/65–74	75+
('000)	6.4	14.0	24.1	22.4	23.8	19.7	12.5

Unemployment Rates	1981	1984	1985	1987
%	10.5	16.2	17.0	16.6

Average Earnings	1981	1984	1985	1986
Male	119.4	–	–	–
Female	95.1	–	–	–

Housing Completions	1981	1984	1985	1986
	443	517	405	273†

Industrial Floorspace	1981	1984	1985
('000 sq. metres)	297.5	293.2	299.9

Employment

Rateable Value 1985	Total	Domestic %	Commercial %	Industrial %	Other %
£m.	14.338	61.2	20.6	5.6	12.6

Local Authority Expenditure	83/84	84/85	86/87
(£'000)	42,174	43,081	52,055e

Economic Development Cost	82/83	84/85	85/86
per capita (£)			
	1.29	1.93	2.11e

– Figures not available

† Only 9 months' figures for 1986

e Estimate

For notes on statistics see p. xi

The island covers 38,100 hectares just a few miles off the south coast and separated from the mainland by the Solent and Spithead waters. The traditional activities are agriculture, tourism and boatbuilding, but newer industries include electronics, plastics, aerospace technology and marine engineering. There are frequent ferry, hovercraft, hydrofoil and air services to the mainland.

Industry and Employment

The economy of the island is largely based on tourism, although recently the expansion of the electronics industry and marine-oriented activities in South Hampshire has had some overspill effect on the Isle of Wight. Sealink is also in the process of investing over £17 million for improved transport links, including new roll on/roll off ferries and terminal facilities.

Tourism is a major employer and this, along with the island's position as a retirement area, has produced high self-employment rates and a large service sector. Approximately 25,000 of the island's labour force of 40,000 are employed in services.

The island's Structure Plan, revised in March 1986, is attempting to encourage manufacturing by providing additional land for industry and warehousing, and the electronics sector is becoming increasingly important.

The population of the island is expected to rise slightly from 119,000 in 1983 to 120,600 in 1991, a rise of 0.7 per cent.

Unemployment is well above the South East average and in February 1987 was 16.6 per cent, representing 7,380 people.

Local Authority Initiatives

Provides land and premises etc. The whole island is a Development Commission Rural Development Area.

See: *Regional Trends in the South East 1985–1986*, published by SERPLAN, May 1986.

Contact: Employment Promotion Officer, County Hall, Newport, PO30 1UD.

KENT

Total Population ('000)	1981	1984	1985
	1,484.3	1,491.7	1,495.2

Main Districts			
Canterbury	122.2	126.6	127.4
Dover	103.5	103.2	102.5
Maidstone	130.8	132.1	132.5
Rochester-upon-Medway	143.7	145.4	145.6
Sevenoaks	111.8	111.1	110.1
Swale	110.0	110.6	110.8
Thanet	121.8	120.1	122.5

Age Structure 1985 ('000)	0–4	5–14	15–29	30–44	45–59/64	60/65–74	75+
	92.7	193.7	343.0	302.6	282.3	178.1	102.8

Unemployment Rates %	1981	1984	1985	1987
	9.1	12.5	12.9	11.7

Average Earnings	1981	1984	1985	1986
Male	138.3	177.5	187.9	200.2
Female	86.5	112.1	120.0	131.9

Housing Completions	1981	1984	1985	1986
	4,550*	6,174	6,307	4,747†

Industrial Floorspace ('000 sq. metres)	1981	1984	1985
	4,548.9	4,383.0	4,308.9

Employment			
Industrial Establishments	1987 = 3,907		
Employees %	–100	100+	1,000+
	67.5	7.4	0.2

Rateable Value 1985 £m.	Total	Domestic %	Commercial %	Industrial %	Other %
	196.479	54.2	19.8	9.2	16.8

Local Authority Expenditure (£'000)	83/84	84/85	86/87
	546,714	551,944	590,565e

Economic Development Cost per capita (£)	82/83	84/85	85/86
	0.62	0.57	0.56e

* Total of district figures
† Only 9 months' figures for 1986
e Estimate
For notes on statistics see p. xi

Kent is the oldest recorded place name in the British Isles. The county covers an area of 373,192 hectares to the south of London. Tourism is a major industry and popular tourist areas include Canterbury, Margate and Broadstairs. Traditional industries are papermaking and cement manufacture, and the county is the UK's principal access to the continent. Agriculture and market gardening are also important.

Industry and Employment

Kent's workforce is employed in the following sectors: manufacturing 25 per cent, services 35 per cent, distribution and catering 20 per cent, transport 9 per cent, construction 8 per cent, agriculture 3 per cent. The manufacturing sector is particularly important in the north of the county, and also around the towns of Maidstone and Ashford. Employment growth has come from newer industries, notably electronics, pharmaceuticals, financial services, leisure and tourism, and the transport and distribution sectors reflect Kent's location and port activities.

Unemployment in Kent is above the average for the South East and acute in certain areas. As a result, development is being concentrated in these areas, four in all, and elsewhere, particularly in West Kent, the policy is one of restraint reflecting the green belt situation.

The four priority areas are North Kent, North East Kent, Ashford and Romney Marsh. North Kent has the largest numbers of unemployed in the county and the highest relative levels of urban deprivation. In North East Kent the coastal area has suffered the most – tourism has declined, there are doubts about the future of the Kent coalfield and there are industrial land shortages. The ports are the mainstay of this area. Ashford has been identified as Kent's growth point and the local authority is encouraging industrial and commercial growth here. Romney Marsh is a rural area with high unemployment levels and poor community services. In contrast, Maidstone is one of the most buoyant centres with low unemployment and a high take up of industrial and commercial premises.

Unemployment in February 1987 was 11.7 per cent, representing 65,678 people.

Local Authority Initiatives

The Planning Department has developed area strategies for the four areas above, along with initiatives on Chatham Dockyard and Ramsgate Harbour. It has also established an Employment Fund, and loan schemes for small businesses. The Kent Economic Development Board was established in 1985. Romney Marsh is a Rural Development Area.

See: *Kent Economic Development Review*, published by Planning Department, October 1985.

Contact: Planning Department, Springfield, Maidstone, ME14 1XG.

Kent

New Town

New Ash Green, a private new town development, was begun in 1967 and now covers 174 hectares. Its planned population of 6,000 has now been reached and most are employed in local services.

Enterprise Zone

The North West Kent Zone was established in October 1983 around Gillingham, Gravesham and Rochester. It covers 125 hectares and in 1985 had 76 establishments, employing 2,900.

Science Park

Kent Research and Development Centre was established by the County Council, Canterbury City Council and the University in February 1986. It covers ten acres and had two companies on site at December 1986.

LANCASHIRE

Total Population ('000)		1981	1984	1985	
		1,385.8	1,379.1	1,380.3	

Main Districts

	1984	1985
Blackburn	142.6	142.3	141.1
Blackpool	149.1	146.0	145.8
Lancaster	125.3	127.6	128.5
Preston	126.4	124.8	124.4
West Lancashire	107.5	107.3	107.5

Age Structure 1985 ('000)	0–4	5–14	15–29	30–44	45–59/64	60/65–74	75+
	88.3	179.5	306.1	270.3	265.2	171.7	99.2

Unemployment Rates %	1981	1984	1985	1987
	11.1	14.0	14.8	13.7

Average Earnings	1981	1984	1985	1986
Male	131.7	161.3	175.5	188.6
Female	86.9	109.4	118.4	128.9

Housing Completions	1981	1984	1985	1986
	4,393*	4,332*	3,672	2,269*†

Industrial Floorspace ('000 sq. metres)	1981	1984	1985
	9,719.6	8,951.7	8,720.0

Employment

Industrial Establishments	1987 = 2,940		
Employees %	–100	100+	1,000+
	78.5	11.5	0.7

Rateable Value 1985 £m.	Total	Domestic %	Commercial %	Industrial %	Other %
	148.995	53.6	19.3	10.4	16.7

Local Authority Expenditure (£'000)	83/84	84/85	86/87
	568,773	556,783	644,781e

Economic Development Cost per capita (£)	82/83	84/85	85/86
	0.25	0.18	0.21e

* Total of district figures
† Only 9 months' figures for 1986
e Estimate
For notes on statistics see p. xi

Lancashire

Covering an area of 306,350 hectares, Lancashire is a county of great contrasts: in the west it is bordered by the Irish Sea; in the east by the Pennines; to the south are the conurbations of Merseyside and Greater Manchester; to the north lies the Lake District. Traditional industries are coal, textiles and tourism, the first two found in the towns around the conurbations while the latter is concentrated in the coastal resorts of Blackpool, Morecambe and Southport. Newer industries include engineering and chemicals.

Industry and Employment

The latest *Economic Situation* report from the County Council uses thirteen indicators of economic performance to contrast Lancashire's performance with that of the nation. The average Lancashire economic standing on all indicators was 9.2 per cent below that of Great Britain and only two indicators – industrial floorspace per head and retail floorspace per head – were above the national average.

It is estimated that there were 482,200 employees in employment in September 1985. Thirty-three per cent were in manufacturing and 60 per cent in services. The number of those employed fell by around 15,000 (3.1 per cent) between 1981 and 1985, but there is now evidence that employment has stabilized and may even be increasing slightly. The bulk of job losses have been in manufacturing, with particularly severe losses in transport equipment, motor vehicles and metal manufacturing. In the four years after September 1981 it is estimated that almost 22,700 jobs were lost in manufacturing, while services increased employment by around 11,600 jobs.

Latest estimates (1987) on the size of the local manufacturing economy put it at £4,955 million in terms of gross output and £2,098 million as net output. This accounted for about 2.6 per cent of national manufacturing output.

Unemployment at February 1987 was 13.7 per cent, representing 77,154 people.

Local Authority Initiatives

In 1982 the County Council set up Lancashire Enterprises Limited (LEL). This independent company provides share or loan finance, business accommodation, co-op support, promotion and training. LEL, in association with the County and various District Councils, has recently produced an ambitious regeneration plan for the towns along the Leeds–Liverpool Canal. Various areas in the north comprise a Rural Development Area.

See: *Economic Situation Report 1986*, published by Planning Department, 1986.

Contact: Economic Intelligence Unit, Planning Department, East Cliff County Offices, Preston, PR1 3EX.

New Towns

Central Lancashire New Town was designated in 1970. Present population (December 1985): 257,000. It covers various sites around Chorley, Preston,

Leyland along with many smaller communities. The final report of the Development Corporation noted that at December 1985 there was 310,000 square metres of factory/warehouse space on several sites and 22,795 houses. 4,200 jobs had been created.

Skelmersdale was designated in 1961. Original population: 10,000; present population: 41,800. In 1985 there were 12,713 jobs in the area and industrial floorspace covered 488,067 square metres.

Enterprise Zone

North East Lancashire Zone was established in December 1983 and covers various areas (seven sites) in Burnley, Hyndburn, Pendle and Rossendale. In 1985, 64 establishments employed 1,900 people.

LEICESTERSHIRE

Total Population ('000)		1981 858.8	1984 866.1	1985 872.2	

Main Districts					
Blaby		77.1	79.0	80.3	
Charnwood		140.1	142.1	143.5	
Hinckley and Bosworth		88.1	91.8	93.3	
Leicester		283.2	281.7	282.9	
North West Leicestershire		79.2	78.9	78.6	

Age Structure 1985 ('000)	0–4 58.5	5–14 115.6	15–29 211.7	30–44 180.3	45–59/64 162.5	60/65–74 92.4	75+ 51.2

Unemployment Rates %	1981 8.8	1984 10.7	1985 10.8	1987 9.7

Average Earnings	1981	1984	1985	1986
Male	131.6	167.5	178.6	194.4
Female	83.8	105.6	112.7	130.3

Housing Completions	1981 3,023	1984 3,516	1985 3,032	1986 2,285†

Industrial Floorspace ('000 sq. metres)	1981 4,904.1	1984 5,015.5	1985 5,047.8

Employment				
Industrial Establishments	1987 = 3,372			
Employees %		–100 80.6	100+ 10.5	1,000+ 0.5

Rateable Value 1985 £m.	Total 119.040	Domestic % 51.3	Commercial % 19.6	Industrial % 13.8	Other % 15.3

Local Authority Expenditure (£'000)	83/84 351,245	84/85 348,088	86/87 384,416e

Economic Development Cost per capita (£)	82/83 0.58	84/85 0.74	85/86 1.19e

† Only 9 months' figures for 1986
e Estimate
For notes on statistics see p. xi

Leicestershire covers 255,293 hectares in the East Midlands. Principal industries are hosiery, footwear, engineering, electronics and plastics, while coalmining is carried out around Coalville. There is also a significant agricultural area.

Industry and Employment

The best estimates currently available from the County Council suggest that employment is around 337,000 (1984) and manufacturing is still the largest sector. This is a net decrease of approximately 8,000 since 1981. The loss of 12,000 jobs in manufacturing, construction and mining has been only partially offset by a 4,000 increase in service employment. Forecasts of labour supply indicate that an additional 26,000 people will require employment in the period 1981–1991, and most of these – 19,000 – will be female.

The latest economic review from the Council suggests that some of the traditional industries recovered slightly in 1985 after periods of decline. There was modest growth in mechanical engineering and footwear, but textiles experienced deficiencies in skilled labour. Tourism is becoming important – the English Tourist Board estimate that at least 6,000 jobs in the county depend directly on tourism – and the county is also important as a mineral producer. It ranks second in Great Britain in terms of tonnage produced and third in terms of value of minerals produced, totalling £131m in 1984, 5.7 per cent of national output.

The revised Structure Plan envisages population growth mainly around Leicester, and industrial development is being encouraged in this area.

Unemployment, although increasing, is still the lowest in the East Midlands and at February 1987 was 9.7 per cent, covering 37,497 people.

Local Authority Initiatives

The Council has produced a Policy Statement on Employment and the Economy and initiatives include an investment programme on promotions, assistance, capital, particularly in the Leicestershire Inner Area and the North West Leicestershire Mining Area. The Council is considering strategies for the long term unemployed and ethnic minority businesses.

See: *Review of the Leicestershire Economy*, published by Planning and Transportation, County Council, June 1986.

Contact: Mr A. Curtis, Economic Development Officer, County Hall, Glenfield, Leicester, LE3 8RJ.

Science Park

Loughborough Technology Centre was established by Loughborough University and the County Council in April 1984. It covers three acres and has seventeen firms on site.

LINCOLNSHIRE

Total Population ('000)					1981	1984	1985
					552.6	556.6	560.3

Main Districts							
East Lindsey					105.4	107.6	108.7
Lincoln					76.5	77.2	78.2
North Kesteven					80.3	81.1	81.4
South Kesteven					98.2	99.4	99.9
West Lindsey					77.5	76.1	76.5

Age Structure 1985 ('000)	0-4	5-14	15-29	30-44	45-59/64	60/65-74	75+
	32.6	71.8	126.3	113.5	109.1	70.1	36.9

Unemployment Rates %	1981	1984	1985	1987
	10.7	13.9	14.9	14.7

Average Earnings	1981	1984	1985	1986
Male	121.3	153.0	165.2	172.6
Female	83.2	104.6	112.8	119.6

Housing Completions	1981	1984	1985	1986
	2,092	2,980	2,757	1,993†

Industrial Floorspace ('000 sq. metres)	1981	1984	1985
	2,419.6	2,466.4	2,365.7

Employment			
Industrial Establishments	1987 = 1,168		
Employees %	-100	100+	1,000+
	82.5	7.9	0.3

Rateable Value 1985 £m.	Total	Domestic %	Commercial %	Industrial %	Other %
	65.761	54.3	19.4	9.8	16.4

Local Authority Expenditure (£'000)	83/84	84/85	86/87
	215,773	208,630	235,874e

Economic Development Cost per capita (£)	82/83	84/85	85/86
	0.06	0.09	0.13e

† Only 9 months' figures for 1986
e Estimate
For notes on statistics see p. xi

Covering an area of 588,556 hectares, this is the second largest county in England and has a variety of rural landscapes and scenery. The Fens and Lowlands lie within it and there are holiday resorts, such as Skegness and Mablethorpe, along the coast. Lincolnshire is a centre for food production and processing and a supplier of grain, sugar and other root crops.

Industry and Employment

Agriculture is an important activity in the county, but this sector has been declining throughout the 1970s and is expected to lose further jobs by 1991. A higher proportion than the national average still works in agriculture but jobs in this sector are forecast to decline from 20,180 in 1976 to 17,000 by 1991. Market towns, such as Spalding, have also grown out of the agricultural activities.

The service sector is the major employer, with 60 per cent of the workforce, and manufacturing is represented particularly by food production and mechanical engineering.

The population of the county grew by 9 per cent between 1971 and 1981, and a further rise of 1.3 per cent occurred between 1981 and 1985. However, the Structure Plan aims to encourage development in the main towns and villages while restricting industrial development in the rural areas unless essential.

Unemployment is above the average for the East Midlands and at February 1987 stood at 14.7 per cent, representing 30,317 people.

Local Authority Initiatives

Mainly the provision of sites/premises. Large areas are Rural Development Areas.

See: *Lincolnshire Structure Plan, Written Statement*, 1985, published by Planning Department.

Contact: Planning Department, City Hall, Beaumont Fee, Lincoln, LN1 1DN.

MERSEYSIDE

Total Population ('000)	1981	1984	1985
	1,521.9	1,490.7	1,481.0

Main Districts			
Knowsley	174.0	168.5	166.3
Liverpool	516.7	497.2	491.5
St Helens	190.2	188.8	188.3
Sefton	300.4	298.7	298.4
Wirral	340.6	337.5	336.5

Age Structure 1985 ('000)	0–4	5–14	15–29	30–44	45–59/64	60/65–74	75+
	96.6	193.9	354.3	280.3	287.3	174.3	94.3

Unemployment Rates %	1981	1984	1985	1987
	15.7	19.3	21.2	19.9

Average Earnings	1981	1984	1985	1986
Male	137.4	173.1	186.3	197.6
Female	89.3	115.7	123.7	131.2

Housing Completions	1981	1984	1985	1986
	3,876*	4,433	4,183	2,813*†

Industrial Floorspace ('000 sq. metres)	1981	1984	1985
	9,022.8	8,583.8	8,301.6

Employment			
Industrial Establishments	1987 = 1,847		
Employees %	–100	100+	1,000+
	78.7	8.8	1.0

Rateable Value 1985 £m.	Total	Domestic %	Commercial %	Industrial %	Other %
	195.909	52.8	21.2	11.5	14.4

Local Authority Expenditure (£'000)	83/84	84/85	86/87
	310,375	x	x

Economic Development Cost per capita (£)	82/83	84/85	85/86
	1.75	2.0	–

* Total of district figures
† Only 9 months' figures for 1986
x Figures not provided
– Figures not available
For notes on statistics see p. xi

Merseyside's 65,203 hectares cover the built up and rural areas on both sides of the River Mersey. Up to April 1986 it was locally governed by Merseyside County Council, but this has now been abolished and replaced by a residuary body. There are five districts in the area, where industries include glass, car manufacture, chemicals, engineering, food processing, shipping and insurance. Agriculture is important and the county also has sixty miles of coastline stretching north to the resort of Southport. Liverpool, covering 43 square miles, is the centre of the county.

Industry and Employment

Recently Merseyside has lost many jobs in port-related industries such as ship-building, transport and distribution, and jobs in manufacturing industry have also generally declined. Encouraged by the government's regional policies, many companies opened branch factories in the area in the 1960s only to close them or reduce expansion in the late 1970s and early 1980s. Employment in service industries has also grown only slowly and many office and service jobs have been lost as a result of the decline of the port.

Food and drink is the largest sector in terms of employment, representing 23.5 per cent of all manufacturing employment. Electrical engineering and vehicle manufacture are also important, with General Motors and Ford having large scale operations in Ellesmere Port and Halewood respectively. Figures from the Liverpool Research Group in Macroeconomics reflect the scale of job losses in recent years. In 1984, 230,615 people were employed in Liverpool, compared to 295,345 in 1978, a fall of 21.9 per cent. All sectors experienced job losses but manu-facturing has been particularly hit – in 1978, 87,550 were employed in manufactur-ing, compared to 47,455 in 1984, a fall of 45.7 per cent.

The county also suffers from large scale areas of urban dereliction and blight, and the Structure Plan aims to encourage urban regeneration through increased land for industry and maintaining population levels. Population has been declining but the rate has slowed, and out-migration has been influenced by the growth of new towns, such as Runcorn, Warrington and Skelmersdale, just outside the county.

Unemployment at February 1987 was 19.9 per cent, representing 134,504 people.

Local Authority Initiatives

Merseyside Enterprise Board, originally set up by the County Council, has invested over £2 million in 35 manufacturers. Funds are also available for co-operatives and small businesses. Most of the districts in Merseyside are beginning to develop economic strategies.

See: *Merseyside Economic Prospect*, published by Liverpool Research Group in Macroeconomics, September 1986.

Contact: Merseyside Enterprise Board, 3rd Floor, Royal Liver Building, Water Street, Liverpool, L3 1HT.

Merseyside

Enterprise Zone

Established in Speke in August 1981, it covers 138 hectares and had 50 establishments on site in 1985, employing 700 people.

Science Park

The Merseyside Innovation Centre is a joint venture between Liverpool University and Liverpool Polytechnic. It covers two acres and at December 1986 had twelve companies on site.

Freeport

Over 600 acres, it is privately run by the Mersey Docks and Harbour Company. It was the second freeport to open, on 29 November 1984, and four companies are now in the zone. The Freeport had a profit of £3.2 million in 1985 on a turnover of £52 million.

NORFOLK

Total Population				1981	1984		1985	
('000)				701.6	714.5		719.1	

Main Districts								
Breckland				96.7	99.6		100.6	
Broadland				97.9	99.4		99.8	
Norwich				126.1	123.7		122.3	
South Norfolk				95.2	98.3		98.8	
King's Lynn & West Norfolk				120.9	124.5		126.0	

Age Structure 1985	0–4	5–14	15–29	30–44	45–59/64	60/65–74	75+
('000)	41.2	89.2	156.2	141.6	140.3	96.4	54.2

Unemployment Rates	1981	1984	1985	1987
%	9.8	13.0	12.8	12.6

Average Earnings	1981	1984	1985	1986
Male	130.7	160.8	176.7	189.0
Female	87.3	108.7	120.1	125.4

Housing Completions	1981	1984	1985	1986
	2,838*	3,735	3,532	2,651*†

Industrial Floorspace	1981	1984	1985
('000 sq. metres)	3,165.1	3,166.8	3,193.1

Employment			
Industrial Establishments	1987 = 1,586		
Employees %	−100	100+	1,000+
	77.2	9.3	0.4

Rateable Value 1985	Total	Domestic %	Commercial %	Industrial %	Other %
£m.	96.135	53.3	21.7	9.3	15.7

Local Authority Expenditure	83/84	84/85	86/87
(£'000)	246,823	241,443	278,718e

Economic Development Cost per capita (£)	82/83	84/85	85/86
	0.14	0.19	0.17e

* Total of district figures
† Only 9 months' figures for 1986
e Estimate
For notes on statistics see p. xi

Norfolk

Norfolk is a farming county, particularly arable farming, of 536,774 hectares. The principal town is Norwich, followed by the seaside resort of Great Yarmouth and the ports of King's Lynn and Thetford. Tourism is a major activity both along the coast and along the Norfolk Broads. Industrial activity is varied, with light industry and commercial and service organizations around Norwich, and older industries include food processing, electrical and mechanical engineering, oil- and gas-related industries and clothing and footwear.

Industry and Employment

In 1981, the County Council estimated that the population would increase to between 730,000 and 740,000 in 1991. This figure could well be reached, as the population grew from 685,232 in 1981 to 719,100 in 1985: a rise of almost 5 per cent. Norfolk is part of the fastest growing region in the country, although population rises are lower than in the previous decade – between 1971 and 1981 the population grew by 10.6 per cent.

If the anticipated population increase occurs an extra 40,000 people will require employment and the labour pool will be further increased by an increase in the resident working age population and the continual steady decline in the number engaged in agriculture – although accounting for 79 per cent of the county's land use, agriculture now occupies only 7 per cent of the county's workforce. Manufacturing accounts for approximately 26 per cent of employment, largely in the main towns, and services/construction account for approximately 64.8 per cent. Rapid industrial development has taken place, particularly in Thetford, associated with the growth inspired by the London overspill scheme.

The Structure Plan envisages growth in the main towns and Norwich is promoted as a regional centre. Given relatively high unemployment levels in the rural areas there is positive discrimination towards these areas and certain market towns have been identified as 'growth centres' for priority in investment and the stimulation of job growth. Tourism developments are also generally encouraged, although there are limits in environmentally sensitive areas such as the North Coast and the Broads.

Unemployment at February 1987 was 12.6 per cent, representing 36,338 people.

Local Authority Initiatives

Mainly land provision and small factory units and workshops. Parts of the north and west have been designated a Rural Development Area.

See: *East Anglia – Regional Commentary 1985/86*, published by East Anglia Consultative Committee, March 1986.

Contact: Mr M. Shaw, Director of Planning and Property, County Hall, Martineau Lane, Norwich, NR1 2DH.

New Town

Bowthorpe New Town is a private development established in 1975 on the outskirts of Norwich. It covers 243 hectares with a population of 5,700. The planned population is 20,990.

Science Park

University of East Anglia Science Park was established in February 1984 by the University. It covers 61.5 hectares and has fifteen companies on site (December 1986).

NORTHAMPTONSHIRE

Total Population ('000)	1981	1984	1985
	532.6	539.8	546.1

Main Districts			
East Northants	62.4	62.2	62.8
Kettering	71.5	71.6	72.0
Northampton	158.8	165.8	169.8
South Northants	64.5	66.2	66.7
Wellingborough	64.7	64.0	64.3

Age Structure 1985 ('000)	0–4	5–14	15–29	30–44	45–59/64	60/65–74	75+
	37.0	76.2	127.8	115.9	98.4	58.9	31.9

Unemployment Rates %	1981	1984	1985	1987
	10.5	11.9	12.8	10.6

Average Earnings	1981	1984	1985	1986
Male	130.9	169.4	175.0	190.3
Female	84.0	108.3	113.3	122.1

Housing Completions	1981	1984	1985	1986
	2,803*	1,810	1,415	2,399*†

Industrial Floorspace ('000 sq. metres)	1981	1984	1985
	2,494.6	2,751.4	2,750.6

Employment			
Industrial Establishments	1987 = 1,679		
Employees %	–100	100+	1,000+
	74.6	11.0	0.4

Rateable Value 1985 £m.	Total	Domestic %	Commercial %	Industrial %	Other %
	78.075	51.6	22.3	14.0	12.1

Local Authority Expenditure (£'000)	83/84	84/85	86/87
	214,607	212,291	246,391e

Economic Development Cost per capita (£)	82/83	84/85	85/86
	0.61	0.90	0.67e

* Total of district figures
† Only 9 months' figures for 1986
e Estimate
For notes on statistics see p. xi

Northamptonshire is an essentially rural county of 236,734 hectares near to the centre of the county. However, although basically an agricultural area, its location between London and the West Midlands and the good communications servicing the area have led to rapid growth. It is emerging as an important distribution centre, particularly due to its closeness to the M1, and other new industries include electronics and food manufacture.

Industry and Employment

According to the County Council, between 1961 and 1981 there was a population increase of 32.5 per cent, largely due to the existence of two new towns and two expanding towns in the area. The latest projections suggest a population growth much slower than in the past. The economically active population will rise from 257,530 in 1983 to approximately 282,700 in 1991.

The replacement Structure Plan attempts to encourage growth in the main centres – Corby, Daventry, Northampton, Wellingborough, plus Kettering and Rushden – to create jobs for the population increase. Certain rural towns such as Brackley, Brixworth, Oundle, Thrapston, and Towcester are being developed as 'rural service centres' where industrial development will be concentrated.

Traditional industries have suffered, particularly in recent years with the notable closure of BSC's steel works at Corby. Other key industries – clothing and footwear – have also suffered losses. However, the latest County Council report suggests that the area is recovering slowly by diversifying its industrial base, particularly through the development of distributive industries in Northampton and Daventry, and by the widespread supply of industrial land. Some 360 hectares of land are available for development, representing eight years of supply, although the distribution of this land is in relatively few locations in the county.

Unemployment at February 1987 was 10.6 per cent, representing 22,881 people.

Local Authority Initiatives

The County Council produced an Economic Development Strategy in 1984 concentrating on marketing and promoting the area, providing assistance through grants and loans, and ensuring the adequate supply of land. There is a Rural Development Area in East Northants.

See: *Northamptonshire Replacement County Structure Plan*, published by Planning Department. June 1986.

Contact: Mr K. O'Shaughnessy, County Planning Officer, Northampton House, Northampton, NN1 2HN.

New Towns

Corby was designated in 1950. Original population: 15,700; present population: 48,000 (31 March 1984). 351,340 square metres of factory space have been completed and approximately 28,600 people are employed in the town and surrounding area. The closure of the steelworks, however, is seriously reducing employment. Unemployment is estimated at 22.7 per cent and BSC (Industry) Ltd are attempting to regenerate closed steel areas.

Northampton was designated in 1968. Original population: 133,000. It was one of the fastest growing areas in the decade up to the early 1980s. The Development Corporation was wound up in 1985.

Enterprise Zones

Two zones are based in the area – Corby, designated in June 1981, and Wellingborough, designated in July 1983. The Corby zone covers 113 hectares and in 1985 had 98 firms, employing 3,600. Wellingborough covers 54 hectares and has 51 establishments, employing 1,100.

NORTHUMBERLAND

Total Population	1981	1984	1985
('000)	299.5	300.7	300.6

Main Districts			
Alnwick	28.8	29.4	29.7
Blyth Valley	77.8	78.2	78.0
Castle Morpeth	49.9	50.3	50.7
Tynedale	54.1	54.8	54.9
Wansbeck	62.7	61.6	61.0

Age Structure 1985	0–4	5–14	15–29	30–44	45–59/64	60/65–74	75+
('000)	18.4	39.5	64.9	61.6	59.8	37.0	19.4

Unemployment Rates	1981	1984	1985	1987
%	11.8	14.1	15.5	16.7

Average Earnings	1981	1984	1985	1986
Male	131.3	160.2	175.5	183.5
Female	83.4	113.6	115.0	123.6

Housing Completions	1981	1984	1985	1986
	916*	998	863	599*†

Industrial Floorspace	1981	1984	1985
('000 sq. metres)	1,277.2	1,316.1	1,322.2

Employment			
Industrial Establishments	1987 = 536		
Employees %	–100	100+	1,000+
	59.6	6.8	0.4

Rateable Value 1985	Total	Domestic %	Commercial %	Industrial %	Other %
£m.	34.247	52.9	11.0	9.6	26.6

Local Authority Expenditure	83/84	84/85	86/87
(£'000)	129,552	120,677	123,018e

Economic Development Cost	82/83	84/85	85/86
per capita (£)			
	0.96	1.37	1.84e

* Total of district figures
† Only 9 months' figures for 1986
e Estimate
For notes on statistics see p. xi

Northumberland

England's most northerly county, Northumberland is the sixth largest in area, covering 503,164 hectares. Agriculture is an important activity, with arable farming and beef production the leading activities. Central government investment in commercial forestry has also been significant. Traditionally, coalmining is the biggest industry, and a number of ports along the coast developed as coal shipping ports. The county has a varied countryside, including the Northumberland National Park and the coastline designated an area of Outstanding Natural Beauty.

Industry and Employment

During the past 20–25 years there have been major structural changes in the economy – jobs in the traditional industries of agriculture and mining have declined and with this decline male employees decreased by 11,500 between 1961 and 1981. On the other hand the introduction of new manufacturing jobs, particularly in pharmaceuticals, and service employment, including tourism, increased the number of women employed by 14,500 between 1961 and 1981. As a result approximately 40 per cent of the employees in the county were female in 1981, compared to fewer than 25 per cent in 1961.

Recent estimates from the Council suggest that employees in employment fell from 93,500 to 90,250 between 1981 and 1984 largely as a result of decline in the mining and construction sectors. Manufacturing jobs held steady and service sector employment increased but at a much slower rate than prior to 1981.

The structure of employment in 1984 was as follows: manufacturing 20,500 (23 per cent), services 52,100 (58 per cent), extraction 9,000 (10 per cent), construction 4,600 (5 per cent), agriculture, forestry, fishing 4,050 (4 per cent).

The Structure Plan encourages new manufacturing employment particularly in the industrial area in the south east of the county. This includes the new town of Cramlington (see below).

Unemployment at February 1987 was 16.7 per cent representing 16,677 people.

Local Authority Initiatives

The promotion of inward investment is a central feature of the Council's employment initiatives. A total of approximately 500 hectares is allocated for industrial development and the regeneration of the Northumberland coalfield area is linked to the development of the local authority new town, Cramlington. A large part of the county is a Rural Development Area.

See: *Jobs in Northumberland – Employment and Unemployment Trends*, published by County Council, November 1985.

Contact: Planning Department, County Hall, Morpeth, Northumberland, NE61 2EH.

New Town

Cramlington is a new town development based on a partnership between the County Council and Blyth Valley Borough Council. Since 1963 the population has increased from 7,500 to approximately 30,000. The planned population is 40,000 by 1991. The town provides a total of 7,500 jobs, of which around 5,700 in over seventy companies are on the industrial estates.

NORTH YORKSHIRE

Total Population ('000)	1981	1984	1985
	677.0	691.1	696.6

Main Districts			
Harrogate	140.7	142.3	144.5
Ryedale	85.6	88.0	88.8
Scarborough	102.4	102.9	103.3
Selby	79.9	83.5	85.2
York	102.1	102.6	102.2

Age Structure 1985 ('000)	0–4	5–14	15–29	30–44	45–59/64	60/65–74	75+
	39.4	83.1	165.1	137.4	133.7	86.0	51.9

Unemployment Rates %	1981	1984	1985	1987
	7.9	10.0	11.0	11.2

Average Earnings	1981	1984	1985	1986
Male	127.5	162.0	175.8	183.7
Female	88.6	111.3	119.7	126.7

Housing Completions	1981	1984	1985	1986
	2,223*	2,719	2,395	1,587*†

Industrial Floorspace ('000 sq. metres)	1981	1984	1985
	2,210.8	2,241.5	2,269.5

Employment			
Industrial Establishments	1987 = 1,268		
Employees %	–100	100+	1,000+
	79.7	7.6	0.4

Rateable Value 1985 £m.	Total	Domestic %	Commercial %	Industrial %	Other %
	80.224	51.7	17.3	5.9	25.1

Local Authority Expenditure (£'000)	83/84	84/85	86/87
	267,191	265,630	290,681e

Economic Development Cost per capita (£)	82/83	84/85	85/86
	0.35	0.50	0.48e

* Total of district figures
† Only 9 months' figures for 1986
e Estimate
For notes on statistics see p. xi

North Yorkshire is the largest county in England and Wales and covers an area of 830,868 hectares. It is largely a rural area, with two national parks – Yorkshire Dales National Park and the North Yorkshire Moors National Park – within its boundaries. Tourism is a key local industry and agriculture is also important. Light manufacturing industry is playing an increasingly significant role in the local economy and major industries are food and drink, confectionery manufacture, vehicle manufacture, textiles and electronics.

Industry and Employment

The majority of employees (over 60 per cent) work in service industries, but manufacturing is also important, particularly in the urban areas. These are mainly in the south around York, Harrogate, Knaresborough and Skipton. Approximately 22 per cent of employees are occupied in manufacturing, and food and drink is by far the largest sector. Nearly 40 per cent of the industrial labour force are employed in food and drink centred on large companies such as Rowntree Mackintosh and Terrys at York. Ten per cent of the workforce is also engaged in agriculture, with many more working in industries dependent on farming for either raw materials or markets.

There were approximately 228,000 people employed in the county in 1985 and the working population of the area is growing at around 2,000 people annually. In its latest *Economic Review* the Council estimates that 2,400 new jobs were created in the latest year, 1985 (5,000 in total less 2,600 jobs lost). From relatively slow unemployment growth in the early 1980s the rate of increase in North Yorkshire is now more than twice the national average rate of increase. The Council therefore suggests that if any inroads are to be made into unemployment in the county a revised target of 9,000 new jobs per annum is needed.

The lack of new industrial buildings of sufficient size in the area is listed as one of the obstacles to growth, although industrial space in general is increasing. Apart from one or two older buildings the county has no supply of factories over 10,000 square ft, although 31 per cent of development enquiries are for premises of over 5,000 square ft.

Unemployment at February 1987 was 11.2 per cent, representing 28,863 people.

Local Authority Initiatives

The latest Economic Development Strategy covers the supply of land and buildings, financial incentives, advice, promotion, visitor strategies, and the development of North Yorkshire as a high-technology base. Special area strategies cover York, Richmond, Stokesley and Whitby. Almost all of the county is a Development Commission Rural Development Area. York District Council also has an Economic Development Unit.

See: *Fifth Annual Review of the Economic Development Strategy*, published by the Industrial Development Unit, North Yorkshire County Council, 1986.

Contact: Industrial Development Officer, County Hall, Northallerton, North Yorkshire, DL7 8AD.

NOTTINGHAMSHIRE

Total Population ('000)	1981	1984	1985
	994.3	1,000.1	1,005.9

Main Districts			
Ashfield	106.8	106.3	106.9
Bassetlaw	102.9	103.7	104.2
Broxtowe	104.4	104.4	105.6
Gedling	104.4	106.3	107.4
Mansfield	100.0	100.0	100.7
Newark	104.6	105.4	106.1
Nottingham	278.2	279.7	279.4

Age Structure 1985 ('000)	0–4	5–14	15–29	30–44	45–59/64	60/65–74	75+
	62.3	129.1	244.2	203.0	195.2	113.5	58.6

Unemployment Rates %	1981	1984	1985	1987
	9.0	12.3	13.4	13.3

Average Earnings	1981	1984	1985	1986
Male	138.4	164.3	174.7	194.4
Female	84.7	107.3	115.7	126.3

Housing Completions	1981	1984	1985	1986
	3,265*	3,475	2,991	2,408†

Industrial Floorspace ('000 sq. metres)	1981	1984	1985
	7,133.7	7,202.1	7,279.8

Employment			
Industrial Establishments	1987 = 1,998		
Employees %	–100	100+	1,000+
	67.9	12.4	1.0

Rateable Value 1985 £m.	Total	Domestic %	Commercial %	Industrial %	Other %
	128.445	48.7	19.2	10.6	21.5

Local Authority Expenditure (£'000)	83/84	84/85	86/87
	438,602	445,043	441,491e

Economic Development Cost per capita (£)	82/83	84/85	85/86
	0.75	1.73	1.36e

* Total of district figures
† Only 9 months' figures for 1986
e Estimate
For notes on statistics see p. xi

Nottinghamshire is a county of 216,373 hectares in the East Midlands. The heart of the county is Nottingham city, and traditional industries are mining and textiles, particularly lace making and clothing. Other industries include telecommunications, electronics, pharmaceuticals, engineering, printing, food, cigarette and bicycle manufacture. Sherwood Forest, Charnwood Forest and parts of the Peak District National Park are nearby, and the East Midlands Airport is ten miles to the south of Nottingham.

Industry and Employment

The county's population increased from 903,000 in 1961 to 977,000 in 1981, and a further rise between 1981 and 1985 now puts the population at around 1 million. However, this pattern of growth has not been reflected throughout Nottinghamshire – Nottingham's population in particular fell from 312,000 in 1961 to 278,000 in 1981, although there was a rise to 279,400 by 1985. In 1981, there were 433,000 jobs in the county, with 40 per cent based in Nottingham. The industrial base is dominated by three key industries: coalmining (10 per cent of employment), textiles and clothing (8 per cent) and engineering and metal goods (11 per cent), and within these sectors a small number of large employers predominate, compounding the problem of dependency. The Nottinghamshire coalfield, which accounts for around 20 per cent of national deep mined production, employed approximately 33,000 people in 1985. It has some of the most profitable and productive capacity in the country but 9,000 jobs were lost between 1980 and 1985. Textiles, clothing and footwear employed 35,700 in 1981, but 5,100 jobs were lost between 1981 and 1985. There is a high proportion of women in the textiles and clothing workforce (approx 70 per cent). In 1981, engineering and metals accounted for 46,000 jobs, but approximately 10,000 jobs have gone between 1981 and 1985. Many of these job losses have been around Nottingham city, as companies such as Plessey and Raleigh have reduced operations. Services have increased their percentage of employment, particularly as Nottingham has developed as a regional centre, and they now account for 52 per cent of employment (manufacturing = 32 per cent).

Unemployment at February 1987 was 13.3 per cent, representing 60,420 people.

Local Authority Initiatives

The County Council has an Economic Development Unit and the strategy concentrates on promotional activity and the attraction of inward investment, financial support for businesses in the form of loan or minority equity participation, property services, and support services for the unemployed. Future initiatives will concentrate on a sector-based approach, following work on textiles and clothing.

See: *Economic Development in Shire Counties, Case Study 2: Nottingham and Nottinghamshire*, published by CLES, January 1987, £1.

Contact: EDU, County Hall, West Bridgford, Nottingham, NG2 7QR.

Nottinghamshire

Science Park

Highfields Science Park was established by Nottingham University and the City Council in December 1984. It covers eighteen acres and 31,000 square feet of building space had been completed by December 1986, with fourteen companies on site.

OXFORDSHIRE

Total Population ('000)		1981	1984	1985
		541.8	555.7	565.4

Main Districts				
Cherwell		109.3	115.9	119.1
Oxford		116.2	114.2	115.0
South Oxfordshire		131.1	133.1	133.3
Vale of White Horse		103.5	106.5	108.4

Age Structure 1985 ('000)	0–4	5–14	15–29	30–44	45–59/64	60/65–74	75+
	35.1	70.7	157.1	115.3	99.4	56.3	31.5

Unemployment Rates %	1981	1984	1985	1987
	7.1	8.3	8.5	6.7

Average Earnings	1981	1984	1985	1986
Male	137.7	180.3	183.0	204.6
Female	89.4	113.9	121.9	140.3

Housing Completions	1981	1984	1985	1986
	2,006*	3,044	2,039*	1,198*†

Industrial Floorspace ('000 sq. metres)	1981	1984	1985
	2,213.8	2,113.2	2,127.2

Employment			
Industrial Establishments	1987 = 1,371		
Employees %	–100	100+	1,000+
	72.1	8.3	0.7

Rateable Value 1985 £m.	Total	Domestic %	Commercial %	Industrial %	Other %
	86.610	51.6	20.5	7.9	20.0

Local Authority Expenditure (£'000)	83/84	84/85	86/87
	187,734	193,708	217,784e

Economic Development Cost per capita (£)	82/83	84/85	85/86
	–	–	–

* Total of district figures

† Only 9 months' figures for 1986

e Estimate

– Figures not available

For notes on statistics see p. xi

Oxfordshire

A largely rural county of 260,786 hectares, Oxfordshire boasts a variety of landscapes including the Cotswolds, the Chilterns, the Wessex Downs, and the River Thames. Farming is the main industry, and Banbury has the largest cattle market in Europe. Industry is represented by a large car factory at Cowley and an aluminium works at Banbury and a variety of light industrial developments. There are also a number of important research establishments in the county including the Atomic Energy Research Establishment at Harwell. The city of Oxford is a centre for tourists, and tourism is an important industry for many areas throughout the county.

Industry and Employment

The population of the county increased by 4.8 per cent between 1971 and 1981 and a further rise of 4.3 per cent occurred between 1981 and 1985. Outward migration from London and the construction of the M40 up to the West Midlands are factors likely to continue this population growth. Oxford has one fifth of the county's population within its boundaries and is the principal manufacturing and service centre. Vehicle manufacture is particularly significant, with British Leyland's Cowley plant near Oxford, and fluctuations in employment here, ranging from 14,000 to 28,000 jobs, have had serious effects on the local economy. High-technology industries are also significant. In recent years, professional and scientific services have taken an increasing proportion of the workforce and now account for approximately 68 per cent of jobs.

In recent years the county has suffered from job losses, particularly in vehicles, but the latest Cambridge Econometrics forecast (1985) suggests that the large shake-out of manufacturing labour is now over and forecasts an employment rise of 18,900 between 1985 and 1995. Population is forecast to rise by 42,500 in the same period, with a corresponding rise in dwellings of 18,600.

Until recently, the County Structure Plan aimed to reduce development pressures particularly around Oxford by restricting growth here and directing it to other areas. However, this policy has been loosened slightly and development in Oxford is now permitted if it can be shown that there is a need for it to be based in Oxford or if the proposal is from a local firm or resident. The green belt area, however, will be maintained.

Unemployment at February 1987 was 6.7 per cent, representing 15,190 people.

Local Authority Initiatives

Additional sites/premises are being made available following the slight relaxation of the restrictive policies noted above.

See: *Economic Growth and Planning Policies in the South East*, published by the Housing Research Foundation, November 1986.

Contact: Planning Department, County Hall, Oxford, OX1 1ND.

SHROPSHIRE (SALOP)

Total Population	1981	1984	1985
('000)	380.6	386.6	390.3

Main Districts			
Bridgnorth	50.4	51.1	51.5
North Shropshire	51.2	51.5	51.9
Shrewsbury & Atcham	87.8	89.3	90.5
South Shropshire	34.1	34.6	34.9
The Wrekin	125.5	128.6	129.9

Age Structure 1985	0–4	5–14	15–29	30–44	45–59/64	60/65–74	75+
('000)	24.5	52.7	92.9	80.3	73.1	43.8	23.0

Unemployment Rates	1981	1984	1985	1987
%	12.5	16.4	17.1	15.1

Average Earnings	1981	1984	1985	1986
Male	122.8	153.8	162.4	176.4
Female	82.5	104.0	107.8	117.8

Housing Completions	1981	1984	1985	1986
	1,881*	1,452*	1,095	1,123*†

Industrial Floorspace	1981	1984	1985
('000 sq. metres)	1,645.5	1,661.0	1,718.8

Employment			
Industrial Establishments	1987 = 1,071		
Employees %	–100	100+	1,000+
	82.5	8.9	0.3

Rateable Value 1985	Total	Domestic %	Commercial %	Industrial %	Other %
£m.	46.709	55.8	16.7	10.9	16.7

Local Authority Expenditure	83/84	84/85	86/87
(£'000)	143,581	146,806	167,843e

Economic Development Cost per capita (£)	82/83	84/85	85/86
	0.56	0.52	0.56e

* Total of district figures
† Only 9 months' figures for 1986
e Estimate
For notes on statistics see p. xi

Shropshire (Salop)

The River Severn runs diagonally through this county of 349,015 hectares. Shropshire has a variety of historical sites and buildings and it is famous for its association with the Industrial Revolution and the development of an early iron industry. Today, the county is largely made up of a number of busy market towns and agriculture forms an important part of the local economy. Shrewsbury, the county town, is the main centre.

Industry and Employment

The industrial structure of the county closely resembles that of Great Britain as a whole, although there are slightly more people employed in the primary industries in Shropshire than would be expected in a rural county. Over the past few years manufacturing in the county has experienced a revival due mainly to the growth of Telford New Town, and service and office-based industries are becoming increasingly important.

Telford originally relied on heavy engineering but in recent years its manufacturing base has diversified to include particularly electronics.

Approximately 60 per cent of the population is economically active and 59 per cent of employment is in services, mainly around Shrewsbury. The town is also developing as a major retailing centre.

The county's population has increased gradually over the years, with an increase of 10.8 per cent between 1971 and 1981. From 1981 to 1985 the population grew by 2.5 per cent from 380,600 to 390,300 and a rise of 6 per cent is forecast between 1981 and 1991. Much of this increase will be in the younger age groups of the working population and nearly half will be women.

Unemployment rates vary across the county, with rates over 20 per cent around Telford and relatively low rates around Shrewsbury. At February 1987 the unemployment rate was 15.1 per cent, representing 21,148 people.

Local Authority Initiatives

Mainly financial assistance and site/premises provision. There are various Rural Development Areas around the county.

See: *County Structure Plan: Alternative No 1 Written Statement*, published by the Planning Department, December 1984.

Contact: Bruce Crawcour, Economic Development Officer, County Council, Shirehall, Abbey Foregate, Shrewsbury, SY2 6ND.

New Town

Telford was designated in 1963. Original population: 70,000; present population (31 March 1986): 110,700. Employment stands at 43,500 and industrial floorspace covers 1,106,175 square metres. The housing stock numbers 42,071. It is relatively successful in attracting Japanese companies.

SOMERSET

		1981	1984	1985	
Total Population ('000)		430.7	440.9	447.0	

Main Districts				
Mendip	89.8	92.7	93.4
Sedgemoor	90.1	91.6	93.0
Taunton Deane	88.2	89.3	90.9
Yeovil	133.1	137.2	139.1

Age Structure 1985 ('000)	*0–4*	*5–14*	*15–29*	*30–44*	*45–59/64*	*60/65–74*	*75+*
	26.0	56.1	99.0	88.2	85.0	58.6	34.1

Unemployment Rates %	*1981*	*1984*	*1985*	*1987*
	7.3	9.8	10.8	10.5

Average Earnings	*1981*	*1984*	*1985*	*1986*
Male	129.7	163.0	176.7	185.4
Female	89.8	113.4	120.9	127.6

Housing Completions	*1981*	*1984*	*1985*	*1986*
	1,979*	2,457	2,356	1,724[†]

Industrial Floorspace ('000 sq. metres)	*1981*	*1984*	*1985*
	1,565.2	1,592.6	1,627.6

Employment			
Industrial Establishments	1987 = 1,468		
Employees %	–100	100+	1,000+
	71.5	6.3	0.3

Rateable Value 1985 £m.	*Total*	*Domestic %*	*Commercial %*	*Industrial %*	*Other %*
	53.992	57.0	18.2	8.1	16.7

Local Authority Expenditure (£'000)	*83/84*	*84/85*	*86/87*
	162,380	x	187,021e

Economic Development Cost per capita (£)	*82/83*	*84/85*	*85/86*
	0.34	0.12	0.06e

* Total of district figures
[†] Only 9 months' figures for 1986
x Figures not provided
e Estimate
For notes on statistics see p. xi

Somerset

The range of scenery in the 345,050 hectares that make up Somerset makes it an ideal tourist location and, not surprisingly, tourism is an important part of the local economy. Agriculture, however, lies at the centre of the county's economy, although there is also a wide variety of industries ranging from cheesemaking to shoemaking and quarrying.

Industry and Employment

A County Council report in 1984 estimated the employment structure of the county as follows: manufacturing 33.9 per cent, services 61.2 per cent, primary 4.9 per cent. Most of these jobs are concentrated around Bridgwater, Taunton and Yeovil. Agricultural production is relatively small, but agriculture is an important industry generating a significant demand for goods and services. Similarly, the extractive industries provide less than 2 per cent of jobs but the county is a major producer of limestone and peat, making important contributions to national requirements outside the county.

The first Structure Plan Alteration document, published in 1985, estimated that the county's workforce would continue to grow to 1996 with employment opportunities also growing but not at a rate to provide employment for the working population in all areas. In 1981 there were 193,400 in the workforce and 172,450 were employed, a difference of 20,950. By 1996, it is estimated that 218,700 will be in the workforce with 185,050 employed, a difference of 33,650.

Most of any employment growth is expected in the service sector and from organizations already based in the county. Small firms are also important: of the 8,000 employment establishments in the county, 5,500 (69 per cent) employ less than ten people and 6,800 (85 per cent) less than twenty.

The Structure Plan emphasizes the need for serviced industrial land to meet indigenous and inward growth and notes that Mendip District, in particular, suffers from land problems and access difficulties.

Unemployment at February 1987 was 10.5 per cent, representing 17,264 people.

Local Authority Initiatives

The Economic Development Unit was established in 1982 and an Economic Development Fund set up, originally with a capital value of £1 million. The fund has been used to develop property for economic development, particularly workshop units, small units etc. The council also carries out a regular review of industrial land, promotional and advice activities etc. There is a Rural Development Area in West Somerset and Frome.

See: *Economic Development in Somerset: Position Statement and Review of Possible Further Policy Options*, published by Economic Development Unit, June 1985.

Contact: Economic Development Officer, County Hall, Taunton, TA1 4DY.

SOUTH YORKSHIRE

Total Population		1981	1984	1985	
('000)		1,317.0	1,305.4	1,303.2	

Main Districts					
Barnsley		225.8	224.2	223.3	
Doncaster		290.9	288.2	288.5	
Rotherham		252.7	252.5	252.7	
Sheffield		547.6	540.5	558.7	

Age Structure 1985	0–4	5–14	15–29	30–44	45–59/64	60/65–74	75+
('000)	79.6	166.3	311.0	258.2	253.2	155.5	79.4

Unemployment Rates	1981	1984	1985	1987
%	11.4	15.9	17.2	18.4

Average Earnings	1981	1984	1985	1986
Male	139.3	174.1	184.4	197.4
Female	84.7	107.3	116.1	125.6

Housing Completions	1981	1984	1985	1986
	3,214*	3,699	3,564	1,842*†

Industrial Floorspace	1981	1984	1985
('000 sq. metres)	7,472.7	6,872.3	6,536.7

Employment			
Industrial Establishments	1987 = 3,986		
Employees %	–100	100+	1,000+
	83.8	7.5	0.6

Rateable Value 1985	Total	Domestic %	Commercial %	Industrial %	Other %
£m.	140.770	47.8	20.3	13.8	18.1

Local Authority Expenditure	83/84	84/85	86/87
(£'000)	243,690	242,569	x

Economic Development Cost per capita (£)	82/83	84/85	85/86
	1.57	1.40	1.51e

* Total of district figures

† Only 9 months' figures for 1986

x Figures not provided

e Estimate

For notes on statistics see p. xi

South Yorkshire

South Yorkshire covers 156,046 hectares, with traditional industries of steel and coal. Up to April 1986 the area was governed by South Yorkshire County Council but this has now been abolished and replaced with a Residuary Body. There are four districts now in the area. The principal towns are Sheffield, a growing office centre, Barnsley, Rotherham and Doncaster; in the latter two are the regional headquarters of the British Steel Corporation and the National Coal Board respectively.

Industry and Employment

Long term structural change, reinforced by the recent recession, has turned the area from a steel to a service sector. In 1971 manufacturing's share of employment was over 50 per cent; by 1977 it was 48 per cent and by 1985 it was around 30 per cent. In Sheffield, the major city, in 1986 manufacturing provided only 58,000 out of a total of 225,000 jobs (25.7 per cent). Steel, which traditionally dominated the local economy, has halved its employment from 54,000 to 25,000 in the last ten years.

Service employment now accounts for approximately 53 per cent of employment, with jobs in finance, banking and insurance particularly on the increase. These sectors have created some new jobs but there is still a large gap left by manufacturing decline. Barnsley and Doncaster have suffered particularly from coalmining decline but newer industries coming into the area include glass, engineering, nylon, plastics, clothing, food manufacturing, microelectronics and biotechnology.

Unemployment is high in all areas and the old county's Structure Plan aims to encourage diversification away from traditional basic industries in these areas. Unemployment in February 1987 was 18.4 per cent, representing 103,780 people.

Local Authority Initiatives

Sheffield has a range of interventionist economic policies and has recently produced an Employment Plan for the city which aims to increase services and create 25,000 jobs. A regeneration project in the Lower Don Valley is also under way, based on the development of high-technology and related industries. District authorities are also developing strategies. Barnsley, for example, has an Employment Strategy updated annually.

See: *Working it Out – an outline Employment Plan for Sheffield*, published by Sheffield City Council, 1987.

Contact: Employment and Economic Development Department, Palatine Chambers, Pinstone Street, Sheffield.

New Town

Mosborough is a private new town on the south east of Sheffield. Established in 1972, it covers 2,226 hectares. The present population is 48,300 with a target of 74,400. 5,000 people are currently employed in the town.

Enterprise Zone

Designated in August 1983, it covers 105 hectares in Rotherham. In 1985, 53 establishments were on site employing 1,100 people.

Science Park

Sheffield Science Park established in 1988 on five acres.

STAFFORDSHIRE

Total Population ('000)		1981 1,018.8	1984 1,019.4	1985 1,020.4

Main Districts

	1981	1984	1985
East Staffordshire	96.3	94.7	94.0
Newcastle-under-Lyme	120.5	118.5	118.4
South Staffordshire	97.4	101.6	103.3
Stafford	117.3	117.2	117.8
Stoke-on-Trent	252.3	249.4	248.7

Age Structure 1985 ('000)	0–4 65.4	5–14 135.8	15–29 235.9	30–44 219.7	45–59/64 200.5	60/65–74 110.3	75+ 52.8

Unemployment Rates %	1981 10.7	1984 12.9	1985 14.2	1987 13.2

Average Earnings	1981	1984	1985	1986
Male	128.4	165.0	175.0	190.9
Female	86.4	107.8	113.9	125.2

Housing Completions	1981 3,871*	1984 3,816*	1985 4,030	1986 2,355*†

Industrial Floorspace ('000 sq. metres)	1981 7,188.5	1984 7,034.0	1985 7,002.2

Employment

Industrial Establishments	1987 = 2,273		
Employees %	−100 70.5	100+ 13.6	1,000+ 1.1

Rateable Value 1985 £m.	Total 130.695	Domestic % 54.6	Commercial % 16.8	Industrial % 13.1	Other % 15.6

Local Authority Expenditure (£'000)	83/84 404,836	84/85 396,295	86/87 432,906e

Economic Development Cost per capita (£)	82/83 0.30	84/85 0.41	85/86 0.53e

* Total of district figures

† Only 9 months' figures available for 1986

e Estimate

For notes on statistics see p. xi

Staffordshire lies to the north west of the Midlands conurbation and covers an area of 271,621 hectares. The development of the county's coal and clay reserves is associated with the Industrial Revolution and today a leading industry is pottery, with the world-famous Wedgwood produced in the area. Engineering, particularly electrical engineering, is also important and this is mainly found around Stafford. Stoke-on-Trent is another industrial area and rural areas include part of the Peak District National Park and Cannock Chase.

Industry and Employment

Since the 1960s the population of Staffordshire has increased from 850,000 in 1961 to just over 1 million in 1981, with a small rise of only 0.1 per cent between 1981 and 1985. There is in-migration from the West Midlands conurbation but there is also out-migration from the North Staffordshire conurbation into other counties. This is highlighted by the decline in population of Stoke-on-Trent from 277,000 in 1961 to 250,000 in 1981, with a further decline to 249,000 in 1985.

In 1981, 489,600 people were employed in Staffordshire but since then job losses have occurred. Important industrial sectors are the ceramic and brick industries, which employ 10 per cent of the county's workforce. It is estimated that 80 per cent of the UK ceramics industry is located within 25 miles of Stoke. However, 10,000 jobs have been lost in the ceramics industry since 1980. Other important employers are coal, construction and electrical engineering, with 3 per cent and 7 per cent of employment respectively. The service sector is relatively small in the county – less than half of all employment is in the service sector compared with 68 per cent nationally. This lack of growth in the service sector can, in part, be attributed to Stoke's location midway between the Birmingham and Manchester conurbations, which has resulted in the city failing to develop as a regional centre. The dominant sector for employment in services is retail distribution, which employs 8 per cent of the county's workforce. The distribution is approximately as follows: manufacturing 44 per cent, services 43 per cent, other 13 per cent.

In the early 1980s the Council predicted that the labour force would grow by 47,000 between 1981 and 1991 due to natural increase and in-migration. However, it also predicted a shortfall in employment of between 50,000 and 133,000 by 1991. Nearly half of the predicted growth in the labour force is expected in North Staffordshire.

A new Structure Plan was approved in 1984, which gives over 1,000 acres of land for industrial development.

Unemployment at February 1987 was 13.2 per cent, representing 52,257 people.

Local Authority Initiatives

Strong land-use focus to policies coupled with the establishment in 1974 of the Staffordshire Development Association (SDA) offering business, development advice etc. Strategy also aims to encourage the service sector, particularly tourism. There is a Rural Development Area in North East Staffs.

Staffordshire

See: *Economic Development in Shire Counties, Case Study No. 3: Stoke and Staffordshire,* published by CLES, January 1987, £1.

Contact: Planning, County Buildings, Stafford, ST16 2LH

New Town

Hawks Green is a private development established in 1977 at Cannock Chase. The present population is 2,000 with a target of 11,000.

Science Park

Keele University Science Park, sponsored by the University, Newcastle-under-Lyme BC, and the county, opened at the beginning of 1987. It covers fifteen acres and has four companies on site.

SUFFOLK

Total Population ('000)			1981 601.7	1984 615.9	1985 624.2	

Main Districts

			1981	1984	1985	
Babergh			74.1	75.8	76.4	
Ipswich			120.4	118.8	118.5	
St Edmundsbury			87.2	89.5	90.3	
Suffolk Coastal			96.5	101.5	103.6	
Waveney			100.0	102.3	103.2	

Age Structure 1985 ('000)	0–4 38.1	5–14 82.5	15–29 141.7	30–44 126.8	45–59/64 114.5	60/65–74 76.3	75+ 44.3

Unemployment Rates %	1981 7.6	1984 10.0	1985 10.0	1987 9.6

Average Earnings	1981	1984	1985	1986
Male	131.7	166.8	186.3	195.2
Female	86.8	107.8	116.9	126.0

Housing Completions	1981 2,752*	1984 3,540	1985 2,857	1986 2,303†

Industrial Floorspace ('000 sq. metres)	1981 2,638.2	1984 2,645.1	1985 2,645.9

Employment

Industrial Establishments	1987 = 1,657		
Employees %	–100 75.7	100+ 8.2	1,000+ 0.3

Rateable Value 1985 £m.	Total 82.754	Domestic % 54.8	Commercial % 19.8	Industrial % 9.7	Other % 15.8

Local Authority Expenditure (£'000)	83/84 222,638	84/85 215,327	86/87 244,051e

Economic Development Cost per capita (£)	82/83 0.05	84/85 0.20	85/86 0.09e

* Total of district figures
† Only 9 months' figures available for 1986
e Estimate
For notes on statistics see p. xi

Suffolk

The county covers 379,658 hectares with 80 per cent of the land area devoted to agriculture. Though not the main employer, agriculture and industries based on it, such as food processing and agricultural engineering, are important. Service employment and electronics are developing rapidly particularly around Ipswich. The ports of Lowestoft, Felixstowe and Ipswich handle over 10 million tonnes of cargo per year.

Industry and Employment

The county is part of the fastest growing region in Great Britain and its relatively sparse population rose by 11.1 per cent between 1971 and 1981. During the 1970s population grew by just over 1 per cent per annum and it is still rising but at a slower rate – approximately 0.7 per cent per annum from 1981 and 1985.

Approximately 55.4 per cent are employed in services, followed by manufacturing at 30.8 per cent (with 44 per cent of this total in engineering and allied industries), agriculture, forestry and fishing with 5.8 per cent, construction 5.6 per cent and mining, quarrying etc. at 2.4 per cent.

The Structure Plan, approved in 1979 and now being reviewed, attempts to slow down population growth and to increase employment to offset existing unemployment and job losses, particularly in the north east, and to provide for increasing numbers of school leavers. It has three main strands: to promote employment where there is a need to increase the range of jobs or offset declining industries, particularly around Lowestoft, Haverhill and the 'small town growth points' of Eye, Halesworth and Saxmundham; to direct pressures for growth to towns on the A45 corridor – Ipswich, Bury St Edmunds, Felixstowe, Stowmarket, and Newmarket; to expand employment in other towns where needs exist, with particular attention to the 'second generation' needs of expanding towns. It is also intended that Ipswich should accommodate a greater part of the county's population growth than in recent years.

At February 1987 unemployment was 9.6 per cent, representing 23,315 people.

Local Authority Initiatives

The Council approved an Economic Development Strategy in 1984 and priority areas selected for initiatives are Brandon, Haverhill, Ipswich, Lowestoft and a Rural Development Area in the north east. A capital fund of £400,000 is available for industrial and commercial projects.

See: *East Anglia Regional Commentary 1985/86*, published by East Anglia Consultative Committee, March 1986.

Contact: Mr E. Barritt, County Planning Officer, St Edmunds House, County Hall, Ipswich, 1P4 1LZ.

New Village

Martlesham Heath was established in 1975 as a private freestanding 'new village' two miles from the edge of Ipswich. It covers 243 hectares and the present population (November 1986) is approximately 2,500. The planned population is 3,500. Most are likely to be employed in the British Telecom Research Centre established nearby.

SURREY

Total Population ('000)			1981	1984		1985	
			1,016.8	1,014.4		1,013.7	

Main Districts							
Elmbridge			112.5	111.6		111.4	
Guildford			124.9	125.8		125.3	
Reigate and Banstead			117.0	117.0		116.6	
Waverley			112.0	112.8		112.5	

Age Structure 1985 ('000)	0–4	5–14	15–29	30–44	45–59/64	60/65–74	75+
	57.7	123.6	225.8	209.3	209.2	120.4	67.7

Unemployment Rates %	1981	1984	1985	1987
	5.1	5.9	#	#

Average Earnings	1981	1984	1985	1986
Male	144.8	189.3	203.5	220.2
Female	94.9	123.8	132.7	141.3

Housing Completions	1981	1984	1985	1986
	2,994*	4,266	4,061*	3,606*†

Industrial Floorspace ('000 sq. metres)	1981	1984	1985
	2,283.0	2,219.7	2,187.7

Employment			
Industrial Establishments	1987 = 2,277		
Employees %	–100	100+	1,000+
	65.9	9.4	0.3

Rateable Value 1985 £m.	Total	Domestic %	Commercial %	Industrial %	Other %
	180.664	59.5	22.4	6.1	12.0

Local Authority Expenditure (£'000)	83/84	84/85	86/87
	340,447	336,312	375,935e

Economic Development Cost per capita (£)	82/83	84/85	85/86
	0.10	0.00	0.08e

* Total of district figures
† Only 9 months' figures available for 1986
# Figures not available
e Estimate
For notes on statistics see p. xi

Covering an area of 167,927 hectares, Surrey is one of the smallest and most densely populated shire counties in the country. Dairy farming and horticulture are important activities and there are many recreational areas along the Rivers Thames and Wey and throughout the countryside. Guildford is the main town and just to the south of the county is Gatwick Airport.

Industry and Employment

The development of the M25 has increased development pressures in the county although the county's Structure Plan largely concentrates on allowing the expansion of local firms rather than attracting new companies. The establishment of small firms is encouraged and industrial development is largely confined to the urban areas.

Service industries account for two thirds of employment in the county but a large proportion of residents commute into London for work. The manufacturing sector is relatively small but electronic and instrument engineering are particularly important. Between 1971 and 1981 employment rose by 1.1 per cent and a further rise of 2.2 per cent, the smallest of any of the South East counties, is forecast by Cambridge Econometrics between 1985 and 1995. Only limited housing development will be allowed, to discourage large scale industrial development and employment growth. Because of the large numbers commuting out of the area, a meaningful rate of unemployment cannot be calculated, so the county is no longer included in the monthly unemployment count. The monthly figure stopped at the end of 1985 when unemployment was 5.4 per cent.

Local Authority Initiatives

Pressures for development have led to a limited local authority role concentrating on providing units for new businesses etc.

See: *Economic Growth and Planning Policies in the South East*, published by Housing Research Foundation, November 1986.

Contact: Planning, County Hall, Kingston upon Thames, KT1 2DT.

Science Park

Surrey Research Park was established at the University of Surrey in 1984. It covers 70 acres, and 190,000 square ft of buildings had been completed by December 1986. Ten companies were on the site in December 1986.

TYNE AND WEAR

Total Population	1981	1984	1985
('000)	1,155.2	1,142.4	1,139.9

Main Districts

Gateshead	213.2	209.6	208.1
Newcastle upon Tyne	284.1	281.1	282.2
North Tyneside	198.6	194.0	193.2
South Tyneside	162.0	158.3	157.6
Sunderland	297.3	299.4	298.8

Age Structure 1985	0–4	5–14	15–29	30–44	45–59/64	60/65–74	75+
('000)	71.8	142.9	269.1	219.7	227.3	138.7	70.4

Unemployment Rates	1981	1984	1985	1987
%	13.9	17.3	19.8	19.2

Average Earnings	1981	1984	1985	1986
Male	131.8	167.8	177.5	193.3
Female	88.9	111.2	122.6	129.0

Housing Completions	1981	1984	1985	1986
	3,629	3,266	3,097	1,439[†]

Industrial Floorspace	1981	1984	1985
('000 sq. metres)	6,381.5	6,041.3	6.009.8

Employment

Industrial Establishments	1987 = 2,396		
Employees %	–100	100+	1,000+
	64.8	9.1	0.6

Rateable Value 1985	Total	Domestic %	Commercial %	Industrial %	Other %
£m.	130.611	50.9	21.1	10.7	17.3

Local Authority Expenditure	83/84	84/85	86/87
(£'000)	184,784	193,054	x

Economic Development Cost per Capita (£)	82/83	84/85	85/86
	2.79	5.54	5.29e

[†] Only 9 months' figures available for 1986

x Figures not provided

e Estimate

For notes on statistics see p. xi

Tyne and Wear covers an area of 54,217 hectares, including the industrial belts around Newcastle, Sunderland and Gateshead, rural areas and coastal holiday resorts. The traditional industries – shipbuilding, coal and steel – are in decline and newer industries are being encouraged to set up in the area. It was locally governed up to April 1986 by the Tyne and Wear County Council, but this has now been abolished and replaced by a Residuary Body. Five district authorities remain in the area. Newcastle Airport offers national and international services and there are ferry services to Scandinavia.

Industry and Employment

Throughout the 1970s and 1980s the area's traditional industries have been in decline – in the fifteen years to 1973, the north east lost 11,700 jobs in mining and 38,000 in shipbuilding and engineering, and these trends continued between 1971 and 1981 when a further 21,955 jobs were lost in the traditional industries. These changes plus the growth in service industries have contributed to a significant shift in the make-up of the local economy. Manufacturing now accounts for only 29 per cent of total employment compared to 37 per cent fifteen years ago and the service sector has grown from 51 per cent of employment fifteen years ago to 63 per cent at present. Industry is also strongly concentrated in the older industrial areas along the rivers Tyne and Wear (two thirds of all manufacturing) and employment in these areas has declined faster than the county average.

The increase in the proportion employed in services has also led to an increase in female employment in Tyne and Wear. Women workers rose as a proportion of Tyne and Wear's workforce from 38 per cent in 1971 to 44 per cent in the mid-1980s, and virtually all this increase was accounted for by part-time employment.

The area also has a large proportion of manufacturing employment in a relatively small number of big firms. By the late 1970s, 50 per cent of Tyne and Wear manufacturing employment was in plants employing over 500 workers and 33 per cent in plants employing over 1,000 workers (this compares with 44 per cent and 29 per cent nationally). Many of the large companies are branches of multinationals, including the recently established Nissan plants. The County Structure Plan aims to increase the range of jobs available and encourage urban renewal. Port-related activities on the Tyne and in Sunderland are also encouraged.

Unemployment at February 1987 was 19.2 per cent, representing 98,057 people.

Local Authority Initiatives

The Northern Development Company has recently been established by local authorities in the area in conjunction with the local CBI and trade unions. There is also a Tyne and Wear Development Company established by the five districts.

See: *Tyne and Wear in Crisis*, published by North East Trade Union Studies Information Unit, 1985.

Contact: Tyne and Wear Development Co, Town Hall, Sunderland, SR2 7DN.

Tyne and Wear

New Towns

Washington was designated in 1964. Original population: 20,000; target population: 67,000; present population: 56,000 (1986). The town's development corporation is due to be wound up on 31 March 1988. At the end of 1985, industrial floorspace completed covered 481,188 square metres and 21,300 people were employed in the town. 16,384 houses had been completed.

Killingworth is a new town development sponsored by North Tyneside District Council.

Enterprise Zone

Tyneside Enterprise Zone was designated in August 1981 in Gateshead and Newcastle. It covers 454 hectares and in 1985 had 249 establishments, employing 9,300 people.

Science Park

Burn Park Technology Centre, involving Sunderland Polytechnic, Sunderland Council and English Estates, established in 1987, on two acres in Sunderland.

WARWICKSHIRE

Total Population ('000)	1981	1984	1985
	477.2	477.7	479.7

Main Districts			
North Warwickshire	60.0	60.2	60.2
Nuneaton and Bedworth	113.9	112.7	112.5
Rugby	87.5	86.3	85.6
Stratford-upon-Avon	100.7	102.8	104.6
Warwick	115.1	115.7	116.8

Age Structure 1985 ('000)	0–4	5–14	15–29	30–44	45–59/64	60/65–74	75+
	28.8	62.9	112.2	100.8	95.6	52.9	26.5

Unemployment Rates %	1981	1984	1985	1987
	#	#	12.8	11.5

Average Earnings	1981	1984	1985	1986
Male	135.8	166.7	186.0	200.7
Female	80.4	104.7	118.2	122.1

Housing Completions	1981	1984	1985	1986
	1,591*	2,023	1,535	1,226*†

Industrial Floorspace ('000 sq. metres)	1981	1984	1985
	2,338.8	2,320.6	2,286.1

Employment			
Industrial Establishments	1987 = 1,709		
Employees %	–100	100+	1,000+
	84.7	6.8	0.5

Rateable Value 1985 £m.	Total	Domestic %	Commercial %	Industrial %	Other %
	71.148	57.9	17.8	10.2	14.0

Local Authority Expenditure (£'000)	83/84	84/85	86/87
	188,555	193,667	203,395e

Economic Development Cost per capita (£)	82/83	84/85	85/86
	0.59	0.63	0.46e

* Total of district figures
† Only 9 months' figures available for 1986
e Estimate
Figures not available
For notes on statistics see p. xi

Warwickshire

With an area of 198,053 hectares, Warwickshire is among the smaller non-metropolitan shire counties. Known as the 'Heart of England', the area has experienced rapid population growth since 1961, particularly around Coventry and the surrounding towns such as Rugby, Nuneaton, Leamington and Warwick. Traditional industries are motor vehicles and electrical and mechanical engineering, and there is a strong tourist industry centred around Warwick and Stratford.

Industry and Employment

Although not really an industrial county, Warwickshire is particularly dependent on the West Midlands, notably Coventry, for jobs, and the northern part of the county has suffered from the decline of the engineering and motor vehicle industries. The main sector in the area is mechanical and electrical engineering, which is the chief business of approximately 23 per cent of companies in the county, but a considerable growth area recently has been transporting and warehousing.

The County Council estimates that the number of additional people seeking work by 1996 will be about 18,600. To add to this, in 1986 about 21,000 people were unemployed and approximately 60,000 were commuting to work in neighbouring areas. Consequently, the prospects are for a widening gap between those seeking work and jobs available. The north suffers particularly, although areas where services predominate, such as Warwick and Leamington, are in a better position and unemployment in the rural south of the county is much lower.

The Structure Plan concentrates on the need for adequate land for development and a total of 385 hectares of land will be allocated in the county in the period 1981 to 1996. Most of this land – 110 hectares – will be developed in the Nuneaton and Bedworth District. New technology industry will be particularly encouraged at certain sites and near Warwick and Leamington twenty hectares of land in the Heathcote Area will be reserved for the development of a technology park. Substantial coal reserves are also located in Central Warwickshire and proposals for opencast coal working will be considered.

Unemployment at February 1987 was 11.5 per cent, representing 21,816 people.

Local Authority Initiatives

Based on the development of industrial land. The County Council, in association with the districts, is spending approximately £8.5 million on the development of 276 acres of industrial land spread across the county.

See: *Warwickshire Structure Plan – Progress and Information Report*, published by Planning and Transportation, County Council, November 1985.

Contact: County Planning Department, Shire Hall, Warwick, CV34 4SX.

WEST MIDLANDS

Total Population	1981	1984	1985
('000)	2,673.2	2,647.0	2,641.8

Main Districts			
Birmingham	1,020.8	1,009.4	1,007.5
Coventry	319.4	313.7	312.2
Dudley	300.8	300.6	300.8
Sandwell	309.8	304.9	303.3
Solihull	198.1	200.0	201.9
Walsall	267.7	264.4	262.9
Wolverhampton	256.6	254.0	253.2

Age Structure 1985	0–4	5–14	15–29	30–44	45–59/64	60/65–74	75+
('000)	177.2	350.5	634.3	509.1	517.4	304.3	149.0

Unemployment Rates	1981	1984	1985	1987
%	12.6	15.9	16.8	15.7

Average Earnings	1981	1984	1985	1986
Male	133.8	170.7	183.9	197.5
Female	87.9	112.5	120.1	128.9

Housing Completions	1981	1984	1985	1986
	8,070	8,254	6,356	3,503*†

Industrial Floorspace	1981	1984	1985
('000 sq. metres)	39,060.1	23,069.1	36,882.0

Employment			
Industrial Establishments	1987 = 11,723		
Employees %	−100	100+	1,000+
	82.1	7.1	0.7

Rateable Value 1985	Total	Domestic %	Commercial %	Industrial %	Other %
£m.	419.387	49.8	22.7	15.2	12.3

Local Authority Expenditure	83/84	84/85	86/87
(£'000)	389,721	329,031	x

Economic Development Cost per capita (£)	82/83	84/85	85/86
	0.20	0.44	0.30e

* Total of district figures
† Only 9 months' figures available for 1986
e Estimate
Figures not available
For notes on statistics see p. xi

West Midlands

Although the West Midlands covers only 90,000 hectares, its population is over 2.6 million, making it the most densely populated area outside London. Up to April 1986 the area was governed by West Midlands County Council, but this has now been abolished. There are seven district authorities. Over a third of the population live in the Birmingham District but large areas are still in agricultural use. The most important industry is motor vehicles, followed by metal industries and engineering. Birmingham is the principal industrial centre and a key commercial and office centre. Other industrial areas are Coventry, Wolverhampton and the 'Black Country'. There is an international airport in Birmingham alongside the National Exhibition Centre.

Industry and Employment

In 1981 total employment was 1,234,230 but by 1986 it was estimated to have fallen to 1,138,620. Since 1979 the area has suffered an unprecedented collapse of its industrial base with the disappearance of an estimated 220,000 manufacturing jobs, according to the County Council. While the most rapid deterioration of industry and employment has been confined to the period 1980–1985, the economy is undergoing a process of structural change which has been evident for at least a decade and a half. The job losses of the past few years can be largely explained by the industrial structure of the area, which is heavily concentrated in contracting engineering, motor vehicles and metal-based sectors. In 1981 over 40 per cent of employees in the area worked in manufacturing and over 66 per cent of these workers were employed in the four key industries of motor vehicles, metal goods, metal manufacturing and mechanical engineering. Engineering accounts for approximately 28 per cent of all employment in the area, metal manufacturing 15 per cent, and vehicle manufacturing approximately 10 per cent. The Structure Plan notes that the county is under-represented in services, although many new jobs are coming from this sector. It aims to regenerate the older industrial areas, particularly the inner cities, and stem outward migration.

Unemployment at February 1987 was 15.7 per cent, representing 207,608 people.

Local Authority Initiatives

Many of the initiatives of the old County Council are now being carried out by the West Midlands Enterprise Board. These include support for co-operatives, a technology transfer centre, a training centre and sectoral initiatives such as the Clothing Resource Centre. The Board has an investment programme concentrating on developing the key manufacturing sectors. District Authorities, notably Birmingham, Coventry, Dudley and Wolverhampton, also have economic development programmes.

See: *The West Midlands Economy, 1984*, published by Economic Development Committee, West Midlands County Council, 1985.

Contact: West Midlands Enterprise Board, Wellington House, 31–34 Waterloo Street, Birmingham, B2 5TJ.

New Town

Perton Private New Town was established in 1974, 1 mile from Wolverhampton. Its current population is 8,700 and the target is 11,400.

Enterprise Zone

Dudley Enterprise Zone was established in July 1981 and now covers 263 hectares. In 1985, 210 establishments were on two sites, employing 3,300 people.

Science Parks

Aston Science Park, sponsored by Aston University, Birmingham City Council and Lloyds Bank, was established in 1983. It covers 22 acres and at December 1986 had 42 companies on site.

Birmingham University Science Park, sponsored by the University and Birmingham City Council, was established in April 1984. It covers twelve acres and had nine companies on site at December 1986.

Warwick University Science Park, sponsored by the University, West Midlands Enterprise Board and Coventry and Warwickshire local authorities, was established in February 1984. It covers 24 acres and at December 1986 had 35 companies on site.

Freeport

The West Midlands Freeport, at Birmingham Airport, opened in late 1986. It is set to be the most commercially viable of the existing sites.

WEST SUSSEX

Total Population		1981	1984	1985	
('000)		666.2	682.7	687.7	

Main Districts					
Arun		118.5	124.9	126.6	
Chichester		98.9	99.9	101.7	
Horsham		103.9	103.6	104.1	
Mid-Sussex		121.1	118.7	118.7	

Age Structure 1985	0–4	5–14	15–29	30–44	45–59/64	60/65–74	75+
('000)	38.4	79.7	142.3	130.5	131.9	98.5	66.4

Unemployment Rates	1981	1984	1985	1987
%	5.7	7.2	7.7	6.8

Average Earnings	1981	1984	1985	1986
Male	132.1	178.7	190.4	207.9
Female	89.9	117.3	126.6	133.6

Housing Completions	1981	1984	1985	1986
	3,112*	3,345	2,942	2,465*†

Industrial Floorspace	1981	1984	1985
('000 sq. metres)	1,670.1	1,737.0	1,724.4

Employment			
Industrial Establishments	1987 = 1,502		
Employees %	–100	100+	1,000+
	58.6	9.6	0.3

Rateable Value 1985	Total	Domestic %	Commercial %	Industrial %	Other %
£m.	105.470	57.4	20.7	8.4	13.6

Local Authority Expenditure	83/84	84/85	86/87
(£'000)	215,922	219,724	250,783e

Economic Development Cost	82/83	84/85	85/86
per capita (£)			
	–0.05	–0.09	–0.01e

* Total of district figures
† Only 9 months' figures available for 1986
e Estimate
For notes on statistics see p. xi

One of the most wooded counties in the country, West Sussex covers an area of 198,939 hectares. Rural areas include the Sussex Downs and the Sussex Weald and along the coast there are a number of resorts, including Worthing and Bognor. Agriculture, forestry and horticulture are major activities but there are also a number of engineering companies in the area and light industry has developed in recent years. Crawley is the main employment centre and Gatwick Airport is nearby.

Industry and Employment

Between 1971 and 1981 the population grew by 11 per cent, one of the fastest growths in the South East, and a further rise of 2.3 per cent occurred between 1981 and 1986. Most of this growth has been through net migration gains taking up employment created by industrial and commercial growth. This has also created a change in the structure of the population – the county now has a higher proportion of young adults and a lower proportion of children than ten years ago.

Of those employed 73.4 per cent are in the service sector, 22.2 per cent in manufacturing and 4.4 per cent in the primary sector. Cambridge Econometrics forecast that employment will rise by 9.5 per cent between 1985 and 1995, following a rise of 12.2 per cent between 1971 and 1981.

The priority for the Council's Structure Plan is to conserve the environment. The original plan considered that previous rates of housebuilding had been very high and noted that sites with potential for office development exceeded those likely to be required by 1991 in most towns. Therefore, the basic policy is to permit new industrial or commercial development only if there is sufficient and appropriate labour supply, so that such development does not add pressure for housing development. Over 30 per cent of the Council's provision for new industrial development is in the Crawley district. In a revised plan in 1985 there was a significant increase in the provision of industrial land and office floorspace, with 238 hectares allocated for industry up to 1996. However, there was a reduction in the number of new dwellings from the original plan. From 1983 to 1996 it is planned to build 37,000 new buildings.

Unemployment at February 1987 was 17,439 people, a rate of 6.8 per cent.

Local Authority Initiatives

Largely the provision of sites and encouragement of small firms.

See: *Economic Growth and Planning Policies in the South East*, published by Housing Research Foundation, November 1986.

Contact: Planning, County Hall, Tower Street, Chichester, PO19 1RL.

New Town

Crawley was designated in 1947. Original population: 9,100; present population (31 March 1984): 72,500. The Development Corporation was dissolved in 1982. The town now has the lowest New Town unemployment rate, 5.8 per cent in 1984. 77,500 are employed in the town and main industrial area in a wide range of industries. Its proximity to Gatwick has also helped employment. Industrial floorspace completed covers 476,900 square metres.

WEST YORKSHIRE

Total Population ('000)			1981 2,066.8	1984 2,056.2	1985 2.052.8	

Main Districts						
Bradford			464.9	464.4	463.5	
Calderdale			192.9	191.2	191.7	
Kirklees			377.2	377.7	376.9	
Leeds			717.6	712.2	710.5	
Wakefield			314.2	310.7	310.2	

Age Structure 1985 ('000)	0–4 137.3	5–14 274.4	15–29 484.0	30–44 407.0	45–59/64 386.7	60/65–74 233.8	75+ 129.6

Unemployment Rates %	1981 10.5	1984 12.9	1985 14.1	1987 13.4

Average Earnings	1981	1984	1985	1986
Male	132.0	164.9	179.2	193.4
Female	86.3	108.1	117.8	127.5

Housing Completions	1981 5,345	1984 4,563	1985 4,274	1986 2,111*†

Industrial Floorspace ('000 sq. metres)	1981 16,862.4	1984 15,323.6	1985 14,943.9

Employment			
Industrial Establishments	1987 = 5,623		
Employees %	–100 72.4	100+ 12.0	1,000+ 0.6

Rateable Value 1985 £m.	Total 222.886	Domestic % 46.8	Commercial % 23.4	Industrial % 12.0	Other % 17.8

Local Authority Expenditure (£'000)	83/84 315,519	84/85 x	86/87 x

Economic Development Cost per capita (£)	82/83 3.04	84/85 1.00	85/86 1.44e

* Total of district figures
† Only 9 months' figures available for 1986
x Figures not provided
e Estimate
For notes on statistics see p. xi

116

This metropolitan area covering 203,911 hectares was locally governed up to April 1986 by West Yorkshire County Council. This has now been abolished and replaced by a Residuary Body. There are five district authorities which include the regional centre, Leeds, and the other major towns of Bradford and Wakefield. The west of the area contains the woollen textile industry and in the eastern section are the coalmining areas. Other industries include machinery, engineering, chemicals, and glass manufacture.

Industry and Employment

Manufacturing, which now accounts for approximately 34 per cent of employment, is heavily influenced by the textiles and clothing sector. This sector employs almost as many people as engineering and has been largely responsible for the high level of unemployment in Bradford and the surrounding areas. In 1981, 75,800 were employed in textiles and clothing, a fall of 31 per cent on the 1978 figure of 109,800. County Council estimates suggest that a further 13,000 jobs have gone between 1981 and 1984. Of the other four key manufacturing sectors, three have been showing employment declines in the fifteen years up to 1985. These sectors are chemicals, mechanical engineering and glass. The only sector to remain relatively stable is food and drink.

In the east of the area is West Yorkshire coalfield, which dominates the travel-to-work areas of Wakefield and Castleford. In the early 1980s, 16 per cent of all jobs and 27 per cent of all male jobs were in mining, but employment has been falling substantially over the last two decades. Between 1961 and 1971 employment fell from 40,000 to 27,000 and it fell again to 23,000 in 1981. By 1984 the figure had reached 19,100.

In the towns of Leeds and Wakefield falls in employment have been less dramatic partly because of the development of significant service sectors.

Unemployment at February 1987 was 13.4 per cent, representing 119,701 people.

Local Authority Initiatives

The West Yorkshire Enterprise Board, established by the County Council, invests in various initiatives in the area. Its latest annual report notes that it has invested £9.5 million in 62 companies, with stakes ranging from £25,000 to £1 million. About 4,200 jobs are involved overall. All the district councils are developing economic strategies and most have established Economic Development Units. The Pennine Rural Development Area was designated in 1984 by the Development Commission.

See: *Economic Bulletin*, published by West Yorkshire County Council, December 1985.

Contact: West Yorkshire Enterprise Board, Elizabeth House, 9–17 Queen Street Leeds, LS1 2TW.

West Yorkshire

Enterprise Zone

Covering three sites in Wakefield, it was originally designated in July 1981. It covers 90 hectares in total and at 1985, had forty establishments, employing 1,700 people.

Science Parks

Listerhills Science Park in Bradford, sponsored by the University, the City Council and English Estates, was opened in March 1983. It covers 11.5 acres and had 26 companies on site at December 1986.

Springfield House Park in Leeds, sponsored by the University and English Estates, was established in June 1983. It covers 1.96 acres and has eleven companies on site.

WILTSHIRE

Total Population ('000)	1981	1984	1985
	525.1	536.2	540.8

Main Districts

	1981	1984	1985
North Wiltshire	104.9	107.7	108.5
Salisbury	102.6	102.0	102.5
Thamesdown	151.6	156.7	159.8
West Wiltshire	100.3	102.6	103.0

Age Structure 1985 ('000)	0–4	5–14	15–29	30–44	45–59/64	60/65–74	75+
	35.0	71.2	133.4	108.5	99.3	60.3	33.1

Unemployment Rates %	1981	1984	1985	1987
	8.3	10.1	10.4	9.7

Average Earnings	1981	1984	1985	1986
Male	131.8	168.1	181.1	196.0
Female	87.2	111.5	123.1	129.9

Housing Completions	1981	1984	1985	1986
	2,631	3,523*	2,786	2,137*†

Industrial Floorspace ('000 sq. metres)	1981	1984	1985
	2,249.7	2,143.2	2,136.2

Employment

Industrial Establishments	1987 = 1,085		
Employees %	–100	100+	1,000+
	67.8	13.6	0.6

Rateable Value 1985 £m.	Total	Domestic %	Commercial %	Industrial %	Other %
	64.946	52.9	21.6	9.7	15.9

Local Authority Expenditure (£'000)	83/84	84/85	86/87
	200,671	195,047	226,455e

Economic Development Cost per capita (£)	82/83	84/85	85/86
	0.63	0.35	0.49e

* Total of district figures

† Only 9 months' figures available for 1986

e Estimate

For notes on statistics see p. xi

Wiltshire

Wiltshire, covering an area of 348,060 hectares, is one of the largest inland counties. It is essentially a rural county: farming is a major activity and there are large areas of chalk downs particularly around the Salisbury Plain and the Marlborough Downs. By far the largest settlements are Swindon, with its growing electronics industry, and Salisbury.

Industry and Employment

The county is a rapidly expanding area, both in terms of population and new buildings, and further growth is expected, particularly around Swindon and Salisbury. Population growth between 1971 and 1981 was 6 per cent and a further rise of 3 per cent occurred between 1981 and 1985.

Swindon is the main industrial centre, with a legacy of heavy engineering, but since the 1970s the town has experienced a rapid diversification in employment. Plastics, pharmaceuticals and food production are now important, along with microelectronics. Its location near the M4 has also increased the demand for office space in the central area of the town. Unemployment has been relatively low but the unemployment level rose considerably in 1986 when the closure of British Rail Engineering Ltd put 2,300 out of work.

In the county as a whole services account for 65.1 per cent of employment, manufacturing 26.9 per cent, construction 5.8 per cent and agriculture 2.1 per cent.

There are three Structure Plans covering South, Western and North East Wiltshire, and the aim is to encourage growth in Swindon and Salisbury and the smaller towns, such as Chippenham, Devizes and Trowbridge.

Unemployment at February 1987 was 9.7 per cent, representing 20,459 people.

Local Authority Initiatives

The County Council provides sites, premises, finance etc. and also runs a business information service. Thamesdown District is running various initiatives particularly in response to the British Rail closure.

See: *Employment, Land and Floorspace*, published by Planning Department, October 1986, £5.50.

Contact: Planning Department, County Hall, Trowbridge, BA14 8JE.

Wales

CLWYD

Total Population ('000)			1981	1984		1985	
			393.6	396.3		397.9	

Main Districts

	1981	1984	1985
Alyn and Deeside	73.0	73.3	72.9
Colwyn	49.2	50.3	50.5
Delyn	65.5	64.7	65.4
Rhuddlan	52.4	53.3	54.3
Wrexham Maelor	113.2	114.4	114.6

Age Structure 1985 ('000)	0–4	5–14	15–29	30–44	45–59/64	60/65–74	75+
	24.5	52.7	88.6	78.6	74.1	50.3	29.1

Unemployment Rates %	1981	1984	1985	1987
	16.2	18.0	18.6	17.5

Average Earnings	1981	1984	1985	1986
Male	135.3	165.6	182.4	191.6
Female	84.5	109.7	111.2	121.2

Housing Completions	1981	1984	1985	1986
	1,569	1,592	1,114	1,091[†]

Industrial Floorspace ('000 sq. metres)	1981	1983	1984
	1,377.9	1,484.3	1,544.8

Employment

Industrial Establishments	1987 = 984		
Employees %	−100	100+	1,000+
	76.5	7.2	0.2

Rateable Value 1985 £m.	Total	Domestic %	Commercial %	Industrial %	Other %
	41.195	54.0	16.2	14.4	15.5

Local Authority Expenditure (£'000)	83/84	84/85	86/87
	163,119	168,521	184,860e

Economic Development Cost per capita (£)	82/83	84/85	85/86
	2.0	2.59	2.05e

[†] Only 9 months' figures available for 1986

e Estimate

For notes on statistics see p. xi

Clwyd

Clwyd covers an area of 242,594 hectares from the North Wales coastline down to the Clwydian and Berwyn mountains in the south. The northern coast has a number of tourist areas, including Colwyn Bay and Rhyl, and inland tourist towns include Llangollen and Ruthin. Large areas of the county are given over to sheep rearing and arable farming and industrial development is largely concentrated around Deeside and the largest town, Wrexham. Coal and steel are the traditional industries; other industries include textiles, aerospace, plastics, chemicals, light engineering and microprocessing.

Industry and Employment

In recent years Clwyd – Deeside and Wrexham in particular – has been hit by the contracting steel and textile industries and towns like Connah's Quay, Flint and Shotton, where the steel plant has contracted, have suffered the brunt of unemployment. Limited steel production continues at Shotton and Brymbo but aerospace is now the leading employer.

Approximately 28 per cent of the county's workforce are employed in manufacturing but this percentage is much higher in the east, which covers Wrexham and industrial areas around Deeside. Service employment is also significant, largely centred on the coastal resorts. However, poor tourist figures and the seasonal nature of employment have not helped this sector in recent years.

The Structure Plan, approved in 1982, emphasizes the need for land to allow for new firms and the expansion of existing ones.

Unemployment at February 1987 was 17.5 per cent representing 23,771 people, and the second highest of the Welsh counties.

Local Authority Initiatives

The County Council promotes industrial development and encourages inward investment, in association with the districts and the Welsh Development Agency.
See: *Abstract of Statistics*, annual. Published by Chief Executive's Department.
Contact: Industrial Development Officer, Shire Hall, Mold, CH7 6NB.

Enterprise Zone

Delyn Zone was established in July 1983. It covers 118 hectares and in 1985 had 62 establishments, employing 1,300 people.

Science Park

Newtech Science Park was established in late 1983 by North East Wales Institute, the County Council and Newtech (Clwyd) Ltd. It opened in 1985 and now has six companies on site.

Welsh Development Agency

In 1985/86 the WDA completed 74,000 square feet of factory space in the county and at 31 March 1986 a further 62,000 square ft were under construction.

From April 1985 to March 1986, £22,000 worth of environmental improvement projects were also approved.

DYFED

Total Population ('000)		1981	1984	1985
		333.7	335.0	335.9

Main Districts

Carmarthen		52.0	53.1	53.6
Ceredigion		61.2	61.7	61.8
Llanelli		75.8	74.5	74.1
Preseli		69.2	70.1	70.3
South Pembrokeshire		38.3	38.6	39.0

Age Structure 1985 ('000)	0–4	5–14	15–29	30–44	45–59/64	60/65–74	75+
	19.8	41.3	74.1	63.3	67.4	46.2	23.8

Unemployment Rates %	1981	1984	1985	1987
	12.7	15.9	17.9	17.4

Average Earnings	1981	1984	1985	1986
Male	129.7	155.9	172.4	178.3
Female	83.9	111.6	120.0	127.6

Housing Completions	1981	1984	1985	1986
	917	1238	694	532[†]

Industrial Floorspace ('000 sq. metres)	1981	1983	1984
	663.7	651.4	637.7

Employment

Industrial Establishments	1987 = 419		
Employees %	–100	100+	1,000+
	79.6	8.0	1.0

Rateable Value 1985 £m.	Total	Domestic %	Commercial %	Industrial %	Other %
	32.538	43.4	16.1	14.3	26.1

Local Authority Expenditure (£'000)	83/84	84/85	86/87
	134,184	141,628	162,273e

Economic Development Cost per capita (£)	82/83	84/85	85/86
	0.37	0.87	2.07e

† Only 9 months' figures for 1986

e Estimate

For notes on statistics see p. xi

Dyfed is the largest of the Welsh counties and covers more than a quarter of the area of Wales. The county area is 576,581 hectares and it has a contrasting landscape: in the north and west are the rural mountainous areas, while in the south east are the industrial areas. Agriculture is the biggest activity, particularly dairy farming, and the main industrial developments are centred around the coalfields near Llanelli. Milford Haven in the south west is Britain's major deep water harbour and oil refining centre.

Industry and Employment

The county as a whole has an inadequate range of job opportunities and the problem is accentuated as the Dyfed economy relies heavily on a few industrial groups concentrated in particular localities. Within the county there are also marked differences in economic structure. The industrial south east is dominated by oil refining, a largely capital-intensive industry requiring a relatively small permanent labour force. The industrial area of Llanelli, based on traditional industries, is undergoing considerable change, and the principal towns of the county are now dominated by the service sector not only in terms of concentration of shopping and other facilities to a larger rural hinterland but also in terms of the numbers of people employed by the public services.

Manufacturing accounts for approximately 17 per cent of employment and the most important sector in employment terms is vehicles, with Leyland in Llanelli as the largest employer.

There are also large fluctuations in the county around a steadily rising trend in unemployment. The industrial south east has figures generally lower than the national average, the south west has the unemployment black spots, and the rural parts generally have figures higher than the national average.

Unemployment at February 1987 was 17.4 per cent representing 20,083 people.

Local Authority Initiatives

Mainly servicing of sites and building small units. Mid Wales Development is the development body in the area.

See: *County Structure Plan, Written Statement*, published by Planning Department.

Contact: Economic Development Officer, County Hall, Carmarthen, SA31 1JP.

Enterprise Zone

Designated in April 1984 in Milford Haven, it covers 146 hectares on 13 sites and in 1985 had 120 establishments, employing 1,900 people.

Dyfed

Science Park

Aberystwyth Science Park was opened in February 1985 by Aberystwyth University and Mid Wales Development. It covers six acres and at December 1986 had six companies on site.

Welsh Development Agency

No advance factories were completed in 1985/86 but, at March 1986, 5,000 square feet of factory space was under construction. From April 1985 to March 1986, £34,000 worth of environment projects were completed.

GWENT

Total Population ('000)	1981	1984	1985
	441.7	439.7	440.2

Main Districts			
Blaenau Gwent	80.1	78.5	78.1
Islwyn	65.0	66.1	65.7
Monmouth	71.5	75.4	76.7
Newport	134.4	128.9	129.5
Torfaen	90.7	90.8	90.2

Age Structure 1985 ('000)	0–4	5–14	15–29	30–44	45–59/64	60/65–74	75+
	27.9	58.4	101.3	87.0	87.3	52.2	26.1

Unemployment Rates %	1981	1984	1985	1987
	13.9	15.4	17.3	16.1

Average Earnings	1981	1984	1985	1986
Male	126.1	163.8	175.5	187.3
Female	86.4	112.6	116.6	130.4

Housing Completions	1981	1984	1985	1986
	1,652	1,566	2,078	1,314†

Industrial Floorspace ('000 sq. metres)	1981	1983	1984
	1,964.2	2,011.3	2,012.5

Employment			
Industrial Establishments	1987 = 1,384		
Employees %	–100	100+	1,000+
	78.1	5.8	0.6

Rateable Value 1985 £m.	Total	Domestic %	Commercial %	Industrial %	Other %
	47.007	45.7	17.5	18.8	18.1

Local Authority Expenditure (£'000)	83/84	84/85	86/87
	187,404	185,644	205,959e

Economic Development Cost per capita (£)	82/83	84/85	85/86
	1.11	0.92	1.12e

† Only 9 months' figures available for 1986

e Estimate

For notes on statistics see p. xi

Gwent

A relatively small county, covering 137,601 hectares, Gwent is one of the most heavily populated areas of Wales. The county contains part of the Brecon Beacons National Park and the Wye Valley and the majority of the county area is devoted to agriculture. The north west of the county, however, provides the main industrial area, with traditional industries such as coal, steel, aluminium and manmade fibres still the major activities. The main towns are Newport, Pontypool and Cwmbran, a new town. The county is often known as the 'Gateway to Wales' and the M5 and M4 motorways connect the area with the Midlands and the South of England.

Industry and Employment

In the period from the late 1970s up to 1983 unemployment doubled in the county, major cause being the shedding of labour in the steel industry and coalmining. Many new jobs are now being generated in high-technology sectors but most of these are based around the periphery of Newport, and unemployment remains high in other areas of steel contraction. Ebbw Vale and Rhonda, in particular, are experiencing unemployment rates around 20 per cent.

Manufacturing now accounts for approximately 33 per cent of employment and engineering is the most important industrial sector. Services account for approximately 59 per cent.

The Structure Plan is awaiting approval from the Secretary of State; it calls for continued development around Newport and increased residential development along the M4 in the south of the county to cope with increased demand from the new growth.

Unemployment at February 1987 was 16.1 per cent representing 27,708 people.

Local Authority Initiatives

Development of new industrial sites and premises. Financial assistance available in steel closure areas.

See: *Economic Progress Report*, published by Planning Department, quarterly.

Contact: Planning Department, County Hall, Cwmbran, NP44 2XF.

New Town

Cwmbran was designated in 1949. Original population: 12,000; present population: 46,000 (1986). The Development Corporation is due to be wound up in March 1988.

Welsh Development Agency

6,689 square metres of factory space was completed between April 1985 and March 1986. The agency contributed £52,000 to environmental improvements in the same period.

GWYNEDD

Total Population ('000)	1981	1984	1985
	231.3	232.7	233.6

Main Districts

Aberconwy	51.4	51.9	52.2
Arfon	54.6	54.4	54.0
Dwyfor	25.9	26.2	26.3
Meirionnydd	31.4	31.5	31.4
Ynys Mon-Anglesey	68.0	68.7	69.7

Age Structure 1985 ('000)	0–4	5–14	15–29	30–44	45–59/64	60/65–74	75+
	13.9	30.2	52.4	42.3	44.1	71.5	19.2

Unemployment Rates %	1981	1984	1985	1987
	14.2	17.5	19.4	18.4

Average Earnings	1981	1984	1985	1986
Male	127.4	159.3	174.5	181.2
Female	–	104.5	–	122.2

Housing Completions	1981	1984	1985	1986
	806	493	686	385[†]

Industrial Floorspace ('000 sq. metres)	1981	1983	1984
	528.1	529.1	529.5

Employment

Industrial Establishments	1987 = 208		
Employees %	–100	100+	1,000+
	77.4	9.4	1.0

Rateable Value 1985 £m.	Total	Domestic %	Commercial %	Industrial %	Other %
	26.234	46.0	17.0	4.7	32.3

Local Authority Expenditure (£'000)	83/84	84/85	86/87
	96,294	102,235	113,342e

Economic Development Cost per capita (£)	82/83	84/85	85/86
	0.80	0.90	1.02e

[†] Only 9 months' figures available for 1986

e Estimate

For notes on statistics see p. xi

Gwynedd

There are many areas of outstanding natural beauty in Gwynedd (area 386,667 hectares), including the Snowdonia National Park, the Llyn Peninsula, the Isle of Anglesey and the northern coastal area. Agriculture is a major activity, with extensive areas of sheep farming in the upland regions. Large areas are covered by forest and slate quarrying is still carried out, particularly in Snowdonia.

Industry and Employment

There is little manufacturing in the county and what there is is largely centred around the towns of Holyhead, where there is a nuclear power station, Pwllheli, Porthmadog, Amlwch, and Llangefni. The largest principal storage electricity generating station in Europe is being built near Llanberis. Manufacturing employment is approximately 12,000, with electronics and electrical engineering key sectors. Food and drink processing is also important.

The range of tourist resorts along the coast have produced a large service sector which is by far the largest employing sector.

The county now has the highest unemployment rate in Wales, with wide variations from relatively low rates around Llandudno to 20 per cent and over in Anglesey.

At February 1987 unemployment was 18.4 per cent, representing 15,062 people.

Local Authority Initiatives

Contact: Economic Development Officer, Caernarfon, LL55 1 SH.

Science Park

A science park was established in Bangor in July 1986 by the University, Gwynedd County Council and Arfon Borough Council. No companies were on site at December 1986.

Welsh Development Agency

No advance factories were completed in 1985/86 but, at March 1986, 11,000 square feet of factory space was under construction. £21,000 worth of environmental improvement projects had been approved.

MID-GLAMORGAN

Total Population ('000)		1981	1984	1985
		541.1	533.9	533.9

Main Districts				
Cynon Valley		67.8	66.1	65.4
Ogwr		130.2	131.5	132.9
Rhondda		82.6	79.8	78.7
Rhymney Valley		105.5	103.9	104.0
Taff-Ely		94.2	93.6	94.4

Age Structure 1985 ('000)	0–4	5–14	15–29	30–44	45–59/64	60/65–74	75+
	36.0	72.5	121.4	108.1	102.5	63.4	30.0

Unemployment Rates %	1981	1984	1985	1987
	14.4	16.9	19.1	17.5

Average Earnings	1981	1984	1985	1986
Male	134.4	165.5	175.2	188.3
Female	90.5	111.3	119.5	126.9

Housing Completions	1981	1984	1985	1986
	1,459	1,204	1,164	748†

Industrial Floorspace ('000 sq. metres)	1981	1983	1984
	2,139.9	2,087.0	2,136.9

Employment Industrial Establishments	1987 = 80		
Employees %	–100	100+	1,000+
	59.2	11.5	0.9

Rateable Value 1985 £m.	Total	Domestic %	Commercial %	Industrial %	Other %
	40.740	48.8	16.9	15.7	18.6

Local Authority Expenditure (£'000)	83/84	84/85	86/87
	229,370	241,990	262,028e

Economic Development Cost per capita (£)	82/83	84/85	85/86
	1.59	2.14	2.32e

† Only 9 months' figures available for 1986

e Estimate

For notes on statistics see p. xi

Mid-Glamorgan

Mid-Glamorgan covers 101,861 hectares, covered mainly by mountains and moorland in the north with main industrial areas in the south. Agriculture and forestry are important in the north while in the valleys around Merthyr Tydfil coalmining is a significant activity. The M4 connects the area to other parts of England and Wales, and Cardiff (Wales) Airport nearby links the county with the rest of Europe.

Industry and Employment

In the last ten to fifteen years there have been major structural changes in the local economy illustrated by the loss of 20,000 jobs in extractive industries, notably coalmining, and the creation of 25,000 jobs in manufacturing and services. Eight coal pits closed between 1975 and 1985 and employment in deep mines fell from 13,734 to 8,425 between 1979 and 1985. Mining now employs only 10 per cent of the workforce, but engineering is also important – approximately 15 per cent of the workforce are employed in this sector. Fifty per cent are employed in services and 32 per cent in manufacturing as a whole.

Recent County Council estimates suggest that 175,000 people were employed in the county in 1984, representing 102,000 men and 73,000 women. Of this total, 15,000 were self-employed. This compares to total employment figures of 179,700 in 1974 and 186,200 in 1978. These estimates suggest an increase in employment over the period 1974–79 of 7,800, equivalent to a job gain of 1,560 per year, followed by a job loss over the period 1979–1983 of 26,200, equivalent to over 6,500 per year.

The approved Structure Plan emphasizes the need for development along the recently completed M4 motorway and provides for increased serviced land in the Valleys.

Unemployment at February 1987 was 12.9 per cent representing 24,860 people.

Local Authority Initiatives

The County Council is mainly concerned with servicing land and building small industrial units. It also has an Economic Policy and Research Unit (EPRU), producing various reports on the local economy, and INDIS, an industrial information service.

See: *Economic and Social Conditions in Mid-Glamorgan,* published by EPRU, County Council, February 1986, £5.

Contact: EPRU, 5th Floor, County Council Offices, Greyfriars Road, Cardiff, CF1 3LG.

Welsh Development Agency

In the year up to 31 March 1986 six factory units covering 557 square metres were completed. Land reclamation projects covering 39 hectares were also approved.

POWYS

Total Population ('000)			1981 110.5		1984 110.6		1985 111.4	

Main Districts

	1981	1984	1985
Brecknock	40.9	40.8	41.0
Montgomery	48.4	48.3	48.9
Radnor	21.2	21.5	21.5

Age Structure 1985 ('000)	0–4 6.3	5–14 14.2	15–29 24.1	30–44 21.5	45–59/64 22.2	60/65–74 14.8	75+ 8.3

Unemployment Rates %	1981 9.4	1984 12.8	1985 14.0	1987 13.0

Average Earnings	1981	1984	1985	1986
Male	119.3	–	–	–
Female	–	–	–	–

Housing Completions	1981 492	1984 499	1985 389	1986 392†

Industrial Floorspace ('000 sq. metres)	1981 296.0	1983 305.7	1984 318.0

Employment

Industrial Establishments	1987 = 224		
Employees %	–100 69.2	100+ 5.8	1,000+

Rateable Value 1985 £m.	Total 10.08	Domestic % 50.8	Commercial % 13.9	Industrial % 8.3	Other % 27.1

Local Authority Expenditure (£'000)	83/84 53,665	84/85 56,323	86/87 69,957e

Economic Development Cost per capita (£)	82/83 0.35	84/85 0.38	85/86 0.45e

– Figures not available

† Only 9 months' figures available for 1986

e Estimate

For notes on statistics see p. xi

Powys

A large upland area, the second largest county in Wales, Powys covers an area of 507,741 hectares and contains a large proportion of the Brecon Beacons National Park. Agriculture, particularly sheep farming, and forestry are the main activities and the upland areas contain reservoirs which supply water to parts of England and Wales. Tourism is also an important industry.

Industry and Employment

Between 1971 and 1981 the county experienced a population increase for the first time this century – a rise of 11 per cent, making it the sixth highest growth area of the 54 counties. It is, however, the most sparsely populated area of Wales and this high growth rate has largely occurred around the main towns, notably Newton and Crickhowell. The increase has continued into the 1980s with a rise of 3 per cent between 1981 and 1985.

Traditional sectors such as quarrying, mining and agriculture offer little prospect of increased employment and the manufacturing sector employs less than a quarter of the workforce. Engineering is the biggest manufacturing sector and services are also important.

The Structure Plan aims to encourage industrial development in various towns in the county with growth particularly in Newton, Brecon, Welshpool, Builth Wells, Rhayader and Llandrindod Wells.

Unemployment is the second lowest in Wales and at February 1987 was 13 per cent, representing 4,745 people.

Local Authority Initiatives

Mainly provision of sites and housing. Powys Self Help is a new agency to aid small businesses and Mid Wales Development is another development agency in the area.

Contact: Planning Department, Powys County Hall, Llandrindod Wells, LD1 5ES.

New Town

Newtown was designated in 1967 covering 606 hectares. Original population: 5,000; present population: 10,500 (1985). Administered by the Development Board for Rural Wales, it has almost reached its target population of 11,000. There was 754,000 square feet of industrial floorspace in 1984.

Welsh Development Agency

No new factories were completed or under construction in 1985/86. £5,000 was spent on environmental improvements in the same period.

SOUTH GLAMORGAN

Total Population		1981	1984	1985	
('000)		389.9	394.4	394.8	

Main Districts					
Cardiff		280.7	281.2	278.9	
Vale of Glamorgan		109.2	113.2	115.9	

Age Structure 1985	0–4	5–14	15–29	30–44	45–59/64	60/65–74	75+
('000)	26.2	50.3	99.8	75.0	73.2	45.4	24.9

Unemployment Rates	1981	1984	1985	1987
%	11.7	14.3	14.2	12.9

Average Earnings	1981	1984	1985	1986
Male	140.2	178.7	187.8	204.5
Female	88.7	113.0	123.1	129.6

Housing Completions	1981	1984	1985	1986
	1,234	1,613	1,556	1,206[†]

Industrial Floorspace	1981	1983	1984
('000 sq. metres)	938.9	938.3	958.4

Employment			
Industrial Establishments	1987 = 1,053		
Employees %	–100	100+	1,000+
	58.1	5.6	0.1

Rateable Value 1985	Total	Domestic %	Commercial %	Industrial %	Other %
£m.	53.553	46.5	23.4	7.6	22.5

Local Authority Expenditure	83/84	84/85	86/87
(£'000)	157,611	160,042	184,460e

Economic Development Cost per capita (£)	82/83	84/85	85/86
	1.76	2.40	2.69e

[†] Only 9 months' figures available for 1986

e Estimate

For notes on statistics see p. xi

South Glamorgan

South Glamorgan covers an area of only 41,630 hectares but includes Cardiff, the major administrative and commercial centre of Wales. A variety of industries, including steel and component manufacturing, are situated in Cardiff and the docks are also a big employer. Cardiff is an important commercial and office centre, and the Welsh Office and related government buildings are located there. Barry is another important town, with a variety of industries, a docks area, and a considerable tourist industry. Penarth is another well-known tourist resort. There are also agricultural areas in the county, particularly around the Vale of Glamorgan, and an airport at Rhoose.

Industry and Employment

Most of the industry is located in the eastern half of the county, while the west is largely unspoilt farming countryside. Until recently the industrial area was dominated by steel and related activities but various closures, including that of BSC's East Moors Steel Works, have turned the economy into one dominated by services. Over 75 per cent of all employment is now in services, mainly centred around Cardiff which is the seat of government for the principality and a commercial and administrative centre.

Government departments such as Companies House and the Business Statistics Office are located in the area, and the property market in Cardiff has been given impetus in recent years by the decision of a number of private companies to move their operations to the area. The Chemical Bank, for example, the sixth largest US banking group, has moved its main operations from London to the area. The Council is also attempting to attract high-technology companies into the area.

The recently approved Structure Plan for the area aims to regenerate the inner city area of Cardiff and allow for large scale industrial developments between the M4 and Pentwyn.

The growth in services has kept the unemployment rate below the Welsh average and at February 1987 it was 12.9 per cent representing 24,860 people.

Local Authority Initiatives

Development of land, sites infrastructure and finance for industrial development. A County Council priority is to improve transport links. Financial assistance is available particularly in steel closure areas.

Contact: Planning Dept, County Headquarters, Newport Road, Cardiff, CF2 1XA.

Welsh Development Agency

No advance factories were built in the county between April 1985 and March 1986 but environmental projects in the same period had £277,000 of WDA finance.

WEST GLAMORGAN

Total Population			1981	1984	1985	
('000)			371.7	364.6	364.1	

Main Districts						
Afan			54.8	51.9	51.1	
Lliw Valley			60.3	60.2	60.4	
Neath			66.9	65.1	65.2	
Swansea			189.7	187.4	187.4	

Age Structure 1985	0–4	5–14	15–29	30–44	45–59/64	60/65–74	75+
('000)	22.6	46.1	81.0	70.1	72.4	47.4	24.5

Unemployment Rates	1981	1984	1985	1987
%	13.4	15.5	16.6	14.0

Average Earnings	1981	1984	1985	1986
Male	135.5	163.9	181.6	191.9
Female	87.4	108.3	119.1	126.3

Housing Completions	1981	1984	1985	1986
	807	972	503	586[†]

Industrial Floorspace	1981	1983	1984
('000 sq. metres)	1,786.4	1,704.0	1,859.7

Employment

Industrial Establishments	1987 = 916		
Employees %	–100	100+	1,000+
	77.3	6.5	0.9

Rateable Value 1985	Total	Domestic %	Commercial %	Industrial %	Other %
£m.	38.594	43.2	17.0	21.9	17.8

Local Authority Expenditure	83/84	84/85	86/87
(£'000)	158,533	162,264	182,412e

Economic Development Cost	82/83	84/85	85/86
per capita (£)			
	0.57	1.06	0.87e

† Only 9 months' figures available for 1986

e Estimate

For notes on statistics see p. xi

West Glamorgan

West Glamorgan covers an area of 81,659 hectares and includes the steel making and heavy engineering towns of Port Talbot and Neath, and the city of Swansea. Traditional industries, such as coal and metal, are still important although newer industries, such as microelectronics, chemicals, car components and clothing are on the increase. Swansea and Port Talbot have dock areas. Rural areas include the hills and forests of the north of the county and the beaches and cliffs of the Gower area and Mumbles/Swansea Bay.

Industry and Employment

The population of the county has declined in the 1970s and 1980s, after growth in the previous decade, and forecasts for the next decade suggest a continuing population decline. The school-age population is expected to continue to decline and the elderly to increase while population in the main city, Swansea, is expected to remain stable. Employment opportunities are the major factor influencing population trends and unless jobs are forthcoming out-migration is likely to continue.

From the end of the war until the mid-1970s the main features of economic change in the county were a continued decline of coalmining in the valleys; industrial growth in the coastal plain; and an increase in the subregional importance of Swansea, which experienced growth in office employment and expanded its range of specialist and commercial services. Since the mid-1970s coalmining has continued to decline but there has also been a very rapid decline in traditional manufacturing in the county. Between 1976 and 1982 approximately 20,000 manufacturing jobs were lost, 14,000 of these in metal manufacturing – mainly due to steel closures, particularly at Port Talbot. Service employment has also remained stable since the mid-1970s, producing a total fall in employment from 159,100 in 1976 to 139,300 in 1982. The sector distribution has changed considerably as well – between 1976 and 1982 extraction/manufacturing employment fell from 40.1 per cent to 31.1 per cent of the total and service employment increased from 59.9 to 68.9 per cent.

The Structure Plan, originally approved in 1980 with proposed alterations submitted in 1984, has allocated land for development particularly around the Lower Swansea Valley and Neath, where steel closures have been particularly acute. At the end of 1985, there were 161 hectares immediately available in the medium term

Unemployment at February 1987 was 14 per cent, representing 22,306 people.

Local Authority Initiatives

An Economic Development Fund was established in 1984 with an allocation of £600,000 to be added to annually as necessary. Fund Finance supports the West Glamorgan Enterprise Trust, West Glamorgan Common Ownership Development Agency and the local ITEC among other things. The Council is also involved in land and premises provision, advocacy, and promotion and advice. BSC Industry Ltd also provides job creation funds.

See: *Economic Development in Shire Counties, Case Study No. 4: Swansea and West Glamorgan,* published by CLES, January 1987, £1.

Contact: Industrial Development Officer, County Hall, Swansea, SA1 3SN.

Enterprise Zones

This was the first zone to be established in June 1981. There is now a second zone, established in March 1985. The two zones cover 714 hectares and in 1985 had 171 establishments, employing 3,400 people.

Science Park

Swansea Innovation Centre was established in July 1986 by Swansea University and the Welsh Development Agency. It covers 3.4 acres, has 20,000 square feet of completed buildings and had six firms on site at December 1986.

Welsh Development Agency

In the year up to 31 March 1986 no advance factories were completed but 23 hectares of land reclamation projects were approved.

Scotland

BORDERS

Total Population		1981	1984	1985	
('000)		92.2	101.3	101.7	

Main Districts					
Berwickshire		17.8	18.4	18.6	
Ettrick and Lauderdale		30.9	33.3	33.2	
Roxburgh		34.5	35.0	35.2	
Tweeddale		13.7	14.4	14.5	

Age Structure 1985	0–4	5–14	15–29	30–44	45–59/64	60/65–74	75+
('000)	5.7	12.6	21.7	19.4	22.9	10.5	8.1

Unemployment Rates	1981	1984	1985	1987
%	7.7	9.5	10.1	10.7

Average Earnings	1981	1984	1985	1986
Male	118.9	–	–	–
Female	–	–	–	–

Housing Completions	1981	1984	1985	1986
	180	471	182	

Industrial Floorspace	1981	1984	1985
('000 sq. metres)	–	–	–

Employment			
Industrial Establishments	1987 = 330		
Employees %	–100	100+	1,000+
	70.4	8.5	

Rateable Value 1986	Total	Domestic %	Commercial %	Industrial %	Other %
£m.	50.3	51.4	19.4	6.1	22.4

Local Authority Expenditure	83/84	84/85	86/87
(£'000)	–	54,238	58,434e

– Figures not available

e Estimate

For notes on statistics see p. xi

Borders

The region has the smallest population of the nine Scottish mainland regions and its settlements are spread across 467,158 hectares between Edinburgh and the English border. The region is unique in Scotland in that no single town acts as a focus for industry and commerce and only two settlements, Hawick and Galashiels, have populations in excess of 10,000. The region is heavily dependent on food production (agriculture and forestry) and on the textile industries (tweed and knitwear), although since 1970 the electronics industry has become increasingly important.

Industry and Employment

Agriculture still dominates the local economy and the principal traditional industry is high quality woollen textiles, woven and knitted. This latter sector is still the largest manufacturing employer in the area, although it has shed a lot of its workforce in the past fifteen years. Much of this labour has been absorbed by the electronics industry which has grown up over the same period. There has been a growth particularly of new small companies engaged in developing advanced control systems and other microelectronics applications, and it is estimated that the region now has the highest concentration of printed circuit board (PCB) manufacturers in Europe. Agricultural and fish processing have also grown over the last few years along with the service sector, tourism and fishing.

Services now account for approximately 52.2 per cent employment, covering 21,000 people, with manufacturing accounting for 31.1 per cent representing 12,000 people. The construction sector covers 2.3 per cent and primary industries 4.3 per cent.

In the entire region there are only ten settlements containing 1,500 persons or more, and representing approximately 58 per cent of the population. The remaining population is scattered and depopulation has been a problem in the past. However, depopulation was reduced significantly between 1971 and 1981 and between 1981 and 1985 the population actually rose by 0.4 per cent.

Unemployment in the area is below the national average and at February 1987 it was 10.7 per cent, representing 4,146 people.

Local Authority Initiatives

Economic development is one of the functions of the Planning and Development Department and it concentrates on the acquisition and servicing of land for industry and the construction or conversion of properties for development. £500,000 is committed to this activity. It also provides finance for small business (FSB) and training, and is actively involved in promoting the region. A section in the department is solely engaged in researching industry's requirements. A study of two pilot Rural Development Areas, South Roxburgh and Eastern Berwickshire, is being undertaken.

See: *Economic Development – Annual Report 1985*, published by Planning and Development Department, 1986.

Contact: David P. Douglas, Director of Planning and Development, Regional Headquarters, Newtown Street, Boswells, Roxburghshire, TD6 0SA.

Scottish Development Agency

Various initiatives are carried out in the area by the SDA, including the provision of premises, advice and counselling and financial assistance. During 1985 the SDA introduced a number of specialist schemes for the rural areas, including Better Business Services, Development of Rural Area Workshops (DRAW) and Programme for Rural Initiatives and Development (PRIDE).

CENTRAL

Total Population ('000)			1981	1984		1985	
			268.1	272.8		272.4	

Main Districts

Clackmannon			47.3	47.8		47.7	
Falkirk			143.8	143.7		143.5	
Stirling			76.9	81.1		81.1	

Age Structure 1985 ('000)	0–4	5–14	15–29	30–44	45–59/64	60/65–74	75+
	16.9	37.1	65.8	54.7	60.5	22.0	14.2

Unemployment Rates %	1981	1984	1985	1987
	12.1	16.4	16.0	16.2

Average Earnings	1981	1984	1985	1986
Male	147.0	183.9	290.3	206.5
Female	85.5	98.6	121.5	

Housing Completions	1981	1984	1985	1986
	100	1,017	943	–

Industrial Floorspace ('000 sq. metres)	1981	1984	1985
	–	–	–

Employment

Industrial Establishments	1987 = 780		
Employees %	–100	100+	1,000+
	79.4	7.6	0.4

Rateable Value 1986 £m.	Total	Domestic %	Commercial %	Industrial %	Other %
	179.0	37.2	20.0	24.2	18.3

Local Authority Expenditure (£'000)	84/85	85/86	86/87
	–	143,719	145,987*e*

– Figures not available

e Estimate

For notes on statistics see p. xi

The ancient town of Stirling is the administrative and commercial centre of the Central region. The region, 262,885 hectares, stretches from the Forth Valley in the east to Loch Lomond in the west, and up to Tyndrum in the north. Engineering, clothing and textiles are major industries but other industries, such as petrochemicals, distilling, brewing, glassware, electronics, aluminium and paper manufacturing are also represented. There are good agricultural areas within the region and the area is also a tourist and conference centre.

Industry and Employment

As in many other areas, manufacturing's share of employment is falling and in the early 1980s stood at 33,700 or 31.3 per cent. Services employed 62,300 or 58 per cent. Within the manufacturing sector, metal manufacturing and chemicals/petrochemicals are the largest employers, with 16.5 per cent and 19.8 per cent of manufacturing employees respectively. Other important sectors are bricks, glass etc. (9.8 per cent of manufacturing employment) and food, drink and tobacco (9.7 per cent of manufacturing employment).

Within Central region is Grangemouth, which is a major port and the location for a large petrochemical complex, centred around the BP oil refinery, which has an output of 9–10 million tonnes per annum, although employment here has been falling. Grangemouth is Scotland's busiest east coast port and it shares first place as Britain's top whisky outlet.

The investment in petrochemicals has been largely capital-intensive and with older industries, such as mining and metalworking, being run down, unemployment has risen to above the Scottish average. Particularly high rates are found in the industrial areas around Falkirk, Denny and Grangemouth, but rates are lower in other parts of the region.

Unemployment at February 1987 was 16.2 per cent representing 19,171 people.

Local Authority Initiatives

Most authorities are involved in site and premises provision and development. The Regional Council has an Employment Premium Scheme.

See: *Central Information Bulletin*, regular, published by the Planning Department.

Contact: Planning Department, Central Regional Council, Viewforth, Stirling, FK8 2ET.

Science Park

Stirling University Innovation Park was established in June 1986, involving the University, SDA, Central Regional Council and Scottish Metropolitan. At December 1986 there was five companies on a site of fourteen acres.

Central

Scottish Development Agency

Various initiatives, including factory building, land renewal and investment, are undertaken in the region.

DUMFRIES AND GALLOWAY

Total Population ('000)			1981 141.8		1984 146.2		1985 146.5	

Main Districts								
Annandale & Eskdale			34.9		35.8		35.9	
Nithsdale			54.9		57.0		57.1	
Stewartry			22.3		23.0		23.0	
Wigtown			29.6		30.2		30.4	

Age Structure 1985 ('000)	0–4 8.7	5–14 18.9	15–29 32.5	30–44 27.8	45–59/64 34.4	60/65–74 13.8	75+ 9.7

Unemployment Rates %	1981 12.3	1984 14.4	1985 14.5	1987 14.6

Average Earnings	1981	1984	1985	1986
Male	123.5	150.1	167.5	173.5
Female	–	97.8	112.7	120.8

Housing Completions	1981 576	1984 618	1985 533	1986 –

Industrial Floorspace ('000 sq. metres)	1981 –	1984 –	1985 –

Employment			
Industrial Establishments	1987 = 338		
Employees %	–100 67.7	100+ 5.3	1,000+

Rateable Value 1986 £m.	Total 76.5	Domestic % 48.7	Commercial % 21.0	Industrial % 7.0	Other % 23.0

Local Authority Expenditure (£'000)	84/85 –	85/86 73,990	86/87 80,602e

– Figures not available

e Estimate

For notes on statistics see p. xi

Dumfries and Galloway

The region, in the south west of Scotland, covers an area of 637,006 hectares and includes a variety of landscapes. A large part of the region is mountainous moorland and most of the population live in the southern coastal plain, opposite the northern English coastline. The main towns are Annan, Dumfries, Castle Douglas, Gatehouse of Fleet, Newton Stewart and Stranraer, where a ferry service operates on the shortest sea route to Ireland. Agriculture is the main activity, along with forestry and tourism, and there is a wide variety of light industry. The service industries also employ a significant percentage of the population.

Industry and Employment

Total employees in the region in 1982 numbered 53,000, and of these 12,200 (23 per cent) were in manufacturing. There are few large scale manufacturing units in the area, with production concentrated in small and medium-sized firms. Services dominate the employment structure with 31,900 employees, 60.1 per cent of the total, and most of these services serve the local population. The population is growing modestly, 0.7 per cent between 1981 and 1985, so the service sector is also only likely to grow slightly. The best prospect for growth in services, therefore, lies in the tourist sector.

Primary industries are also important, accounting for 6,000 employees, 11.3 per cent of employment, and forestry is one of the few industries which offer the prospect of increased employment in the area. Over 22 per cent of the region's land area is planted and production is forecast to increase more than twofold in the next fifteen years. Increased productivity and technology will restrict job potential but the Council forecasts an increase in direct employment of 3 per cent over the next five years and during the following decade the increase is estimated at just under 3 per cent per annum.

The Structure Plan highlights four areas where industrial development should be concentrated – Wigtown District and Upper Nithsdale, where high levels of unemployment prevail, and Lower Nithsdale and Lower Annandale, where prospects for industrial growth are highest. The unemployment rate is just under the Scottish average and rates are particularly low in the Dumfries area. In other areas, particularly to the west of the region, rates are much higher – between 20 and 25 per cent in Newton Stewart and the former mining areas of Kirconnel and Sanquhar.

Unemployment at February 1987 was 14.6 per cent representing 8,519 people.

Local Authority Initiatives

In 1986 the Regional Council established a new Department of Economic Development. The Department has published a study of forest resources and related industry in the region and other studies will follow. The Council is also active in site, premises provision, promotion and providing finance. In Wigtown, the Wigtown Rural Development Company has been established.

See: *Dumfries and Galloway Structure Plan, Written Statement*, published by the Planning Department, 1985.

Contact: Leslie Jardine, Director of Economic Development, Dumfries and Galloway Regional Council, 118 English Street, Dumfries, DG1 2DE.

Scottish Development Agency

Involved in a range of initiatives, including the Wigtown Development Co.

FIFE

Total Population ('000)			1981 325.0	1984 344.5		1985 344.0	

Main Districts

			1981	1984		1985	
Dunfermline			122.0	128.8		129.1	
Kirkcaldy			142.7	149.4		148.8	
North East Fife			60.2	66.2		66.0	

Age Structure 1985 ('000)	0–4 22.3	5–14 45.9	15–29 83.0	30–44 68.8	45–59/64 73.8	60/65–74 29.2	75+ 20.1

Unemployment Rates %	1981 11.9	1984 14.0	1985 15.4	1987 16.7

Average Earnings	1981	1984	1985	1986
Male	134.2	174.6	185.5	195.9
Female	88.4	106.6	117.3	125.7

Housing Completions	1981 852	1984 1,271	1985 1,115	1986 –

Industrial Floorspace ('000 sq. metres)	1981 –	1984 –	1985 –

Employment

Industrial Establishments	1987 = 508		
Employees %	–100 68.3	100+ 12.1	1,000+ 0.6

Rateable Value 1986 £m.	Total 232.3	Domestic % 37.7	Commercial % 19.2	Industrial % 21.8	Other % 21.1

Local Authority Expenditure (£'000)	84/85 –	85/86 182,101	86/87 192,019e

– Figures not available
e Estimate
For notes on statistics see p. xi

The region is located in the East of Scotland and is almost surrounded by water: on the north by the Firth of Tay, on the east by the North Sea and on the south by the Firth of Forth. It covers an area of 130,698 hectares and of that approximately 73.4 per cent (96,000 hectares) is agricultural land.

Traditionally coalmining was an important industry, but newer industries include electronics, engineering, metal fabrication, oil and chemicals. The major towns are Glenrothes, Kirkcaldy, Dunfermline, Buckhaven, Methil, St Andrews, Rosyth and Cowdenbeath.

Industry and Employment

The total workforce numbers 135,000 and 53.5 per cent are employed in services, 33 per cent in manufacturing, 7 per cent in construction and 6.5 per cent in primary industries. In manufacturing, approximately two-thirds are employed in engineering and allied trades. Engineering and electronics are particularly predominant in Fife and in the 1970s Fife experienced employment growth particularly as a result of its success in attracting electronic firms and offshore oil engineering fabrication, which offset the decline in traditional industries such as coalmining. Estimates suggest that 20 per cent of the country's electronic industry employment is in Fife.

The development of electronics has also brought overseas companies to the area – in 1983 there were 37 overseas-owned plants, employing 19 per cent of the region's workforce.

Unemployment is above the Scottish mainland average and at February 1987 was 16.7 per cent representing 22,669 people.

Local Authority Initiatives

The Regional Council is expanding services, notably in education and social services, to create jobs. Financial assistance for small firms, new start ups etc. is also available.

See: *Strategic Projections 5*, published by Economic Development and Planning, 1986.

Contact: Planning Dept, Fife House, Glenrothes, KY7 5LT.

New Towns

Glenrothes was designated in 1984. Original population: 1,100; present population (31 March 1985): 38,000. 16,767 people are employed in the town and industrial floorspace covers 238,003 square metres. The town is at the heart of the Fife region and is now also the administrative capital, with most of the Regional Council's departments located there.

Fife

Dalgety Bay is a private new town development near Dunfermline. The population is 7,000 and two large industrial estates are sited nearby.

Science Park

St Andrews Centre was opened in December 1984 by the University and the Scottish Development Agency. By December 1986, two companies were on the site of 0.74 acres.

Scottish Development Agency

Various investment and development activities in the region.

GRAMPIAN

Total Population ('000)	1981	1984	1985
	462.8	497.3	500.5

Main Districts	1981	1984	1985
Aberdeen	199.8	214.0	215.2
Banff and Buchan	80.1	83.2	83.3
Gordon	61.7	68.7	70.1
Kincardine & Deeside	41.0	45.6	46.7
Moray	80.1	85.5	85.0

Age Structure 1985 ('000)	0–4	5–14	15–29	30–44	45–59/64	60/65–74	75+
	31.9	67.1	124.3	103.6	103.9	38.6	29.9

Unemployment Rates %	1981	1984	1985	1987
	7.4	9.3	8.4	11.1

Average Earnings	1981	1984	1985	1986
Male	152.7	209.1	220.0	237.4
Female	93.5	113.4	122.9	133.5

Housing Completions	1981	1984	1985	1986
	2,958	3,334	3,277	–

Industrial Floorspace ('000 sq. metres)	1981	1984	1985
	–	–	–

Employment

Industrial Establishments	1987 = 1,616		
Employees %	–100	100+	1,000+
	71.3	8.5	0.3

Rateable Value 1986 £m.	Total	Domestic %	Commercial %	Industrial %	Other %
	348.9	36.3	31.3	11.0	21.1

Local Authority Expenditure (£'000)	84/85	85/86	86/87
	–	252,602	276,732e

– Figures not available
e Estimate
For notes on statistics see p. xi

Grampian

The centre of this region, which covers 870,384 hectares in the north east of Scotland, is Aberdeen. Offshore oil developments have had a significant impact on the area in recent years, and Aberdeen and Peterhead have become the major administrative, service and supply centres for these developments. In the non-oil sector the region supports a variety of industries including agriculture, fishing, distilling, textiles, marine engineering, food processing and papermaking. The region also has a varied topography, including the Cairngorms.

Industry and Employment

Up until the mid-1960s, when oil was commercially developed in the North Sea, the region suffered from migration and population loss. However, by the start of 1981 the offshore oil and gas industries had brought an influx of 600 new companies, providing 35,900 jobs. The latest Regional Council forecasts put oil-related employment at 49,000 in 1986 and suggest that it will rise to 52,500 in 2001 after peaking at 55,000 in 1996. It accounts for only 20 per cent of employment in the region but its fortunes clearly have an impact on other sectors such as engineering, construction etc. Uncertainty in the oil industry resulting from lower oil prices can have sudden effects on the economy and a recent study by the Royal Bank of Scotland suggests that the recent oil price fall could cost 18,000 direct jobs in Scotland in 1988, most of which would be in Grampian.

In the non-oil economy, employment in 1986 was 165,500, compared to 168,000 in 1981. It is forecast to rise to 168,600 by 1996 with a fall to 167,540 by 2001. Services dominated the employment structure in 1986, with 69.6 per cent of employment, compared to 65.9 per cent in 1981. Manufacturing accounted for 16.5 per cent (19 per cent in 1981), construction 8.8 per cent (9.7 per cent in 1981), primary industries 4.9 per cent (5.3 per cent in 1981).

Most of the new jobs forecast are expected to be in the Aberdeen area, where the population is forecast to grow by 19,300 between 1986 and 2001. More people are also expected to continue to move into Grampian than move out, a total of 11,000 more between 1986 and 2001, because of better job opportunities than in the rest of the country.

Unemployment is relatively low in Aberdeen but is a more serious problem in the north of the region and in Forres particularly. At February 1987 the rate was 11.1 per cent, representing 25,013 people.

Local Authority Initiatives

NESDA, the North East Scotland Development Authority, is the development and promotional body of the Regional Council's Development Department. Local Authorities provide sites/finance for industrial development. The Regional Council produces annual forecasts for employment, population, housing.

See: *Strategic Forecasts: Employment, Population, Housing, 1986 Update*, published by Department of Physical Planning, 1986.

158

Contact: Department of Physical Planning, Woodhill House, Ashgrove Road West, Aberdeen, AB9 2LU.

New Town

Westhill New Town is a private development four miles from Aberdeen. The population is 8,500, with a target of 9,000.

Science Park

Aberdeen Science and Research Park opened in 1987, sponsored by Aberdeen University, SDA, Grampian Regional Council and Robert Gordon Institute of Technology.

Scottish Development Agency

The SDA has an investment portfolio of £4.4 million in Grampian.

HIGHLAND

Total Population ('000)			1981	1984	1985	
			187.0	197.2	198.6	

Main Districts						
Caithness			26.9	27.4	27.3	
Inverness			54.2	58.3	58.8	
Lochaber			19.0	19.3	19.4	
Ross & Cromarty			44.8	47.4	47.8	
Skye & Lochalsh			9.9	11.0	11.3	
Sutherland			12.9	13.2	13.2	

Age Structure 1985 ('000)	0–4	5–14	15–29	30–44	45–59/64	60/65–74	75+
	13.6	28.3	45.0	40.6	42.7	15.7	11.8

Unemployment Rates %	1981	1984	1985	1987
	11.3	15.4	17.3	17.8

Average Earnings	1981	1984	1985	1986
Male	145.3	184.6	182.8	201.2
Female	83.6	112.5	113.8	123.5

Housing Completions	1981	1984	1985	1986
	1125	1055	994	–

Industrial Floorspace ('000 sq. metres)	1981	1984	1985
	–	–	–

Employment
Industrial Establishments 1987 = 838

Employees %	–100	100+	1,000+
	74.0	4.0	0.1

Rateable Value 1986 £m.	Total	Domestic %	Commercial %	Industrial %	Other %
	116.2	37.6	28.3	13.5	20.2

Local Authority Expenditure (£'000)	84/85	85/86	86/87
	–	126,194	135,266e

- Figures not available
e Estimate
For notes on statistics see p. xi

Covering 2,538,831 hectares, the region takes up a third of the Scottish land surface and much of the region is sparsely populated, sometimes uninhabited, mountains and moorland. Notable scenic attractions include Ben Nevis, the highest peak in the United Kingdom, and Loch Ness. Economic development has largely centred around rural activities such as agriculture, fishing, forestry, crofting and tourism. There are some large industrial developments in certain places, such as a nuclear power plant at Caithness, aluminium smelting at Invergordon, Fort William and Kinlochleven, paper and pulp industries at Fort William and oil platform construction in certain areas. Inverness is the principal administrative and tourist centre and it is also the home of the headquarters of the Highlands and Islands Development Board.

Industry and Employment

A large part of the region is mountainous and remote from the main centres of population and land and sea communications are difficult. These factors, along with the problems of distance and cost, make the area unsuitable for many forms of manufacturing, although there are opportunities for processing of primary products. Tourism is also an important sector, but employment in traditional industries such as agriculture has been declining, and, until recently, the region had a long history of depopulation. Between 1981 and 1985, however, the population rose by 1.5 per cent.

Approximately 120,000 people are employed in the area, with 65.5 per cent employed in services, 14 per cent in manufacturing, 10.2 per cent in construction, 9 per cent in primary industries, and the remainder in utilities. Agriculture employs approximately 5,000 (4.3 per cent of the total.) Offshore-related activities are major employers: there are four platform fabrication yards in the region. Construction is also an important sector, although there has been a fall in orders in the last two years – the shortage of major civil engineering contracts, low levels of housebuilding and reduced grants for housing improvements have all contributed to this fall. The latest hotel occupancy survey, for 1985, confirms that 1985 was the best year for tourism since 1977 and the tonnage and value of fish landings was also up on previous years.

Unemployment is relatively high in most areas and at February 1987 was 17.8 per cent, representing 14,976 people.

Local Authority Initiatives

Local authorities work closely with the Highlands and Islands Development Board (HIDB) to encourage indigenous industry and provide sites and premises, key worker housing and loans and grants.

See: *Annual Report, Highlands and Islands Development Board*, published by HIDB, 1986.

Contact: HIDB, Bridge House, 27 Bank Street, Inverness, 1V1 QR

Highland

Enterprise Zone

Designated in October 1983 at Invergordon, it covers 60 hectares on two sites. In 1985 twenty-two establishments were on site employing 200 people.

Highlands and Islands Development Board (HIDB)

Various initiatives in the area, including land developments, tourism projects, fisheries, industrial development and social projects.

LOTHIAN

Total Population		1981	1984	1985	
('000)		723.1	744.6	745.2	

Main Districts					
East Lothian		78.9	81.3	82.1	
Edinburgh		425.2	439.7	439.6	
Midlothian		81.6	81.9	81.45	
West Lothian		137.2	141.5	141.94	

Age Structure 1985	0–4	5–14	15–29	30–44	45–59/64	60/65–74	75+
('000)	43.5	89.7	192.4	149.0	161.1	62.1	46.6

Unemployment Rates	1981	1984	1985	1987
%	9.7	12.9	12.7	13.2

Average Earnings	1981	1984	1985	1986
Male	145.3	176.7	189.8	202.1
Female	91.0	117.5	123.7	132.1

Housing Completions	1981	1984	1985	1986
	–	2,769	2,736	–

Industrial Floorspace	1981	1984	1985
('000 sq. metres)	–	–	–

Employment			
Industrial Establishments	1987 = 1,526		
Employees %	–100	100+	1,000+
	79.7	8.6	0.6

Rateable Value 1986	Total	Domestic %	Commercial %	Industrial %	Other %
£m.	513.0	43.5	29.8	5.9	20.6

Local Authority Expenditure	84/85	85/86	86/87
(£'000)	–	399,242	429,360e

– Figures not available

e Estimate

For notes on statistics see p. xi

Lothian

This region, covering 175,509 hectares, is located in the south east of Scotland, bounded on the north by the Firth of Forth, and on the east by the North Sea. Edinburgh is the main service centre, with banking and insurance particularly predominant, and it is also the government and legal centre for Scotland. Industry is well represented, with light and heavy engineering, electronics, food processing and oil-related services particularly important. Elsewhere in the region agriculture is a key activity, and in the west of the region is Livingston New Town.

Industry and Employment

The region's employment is dominated by the service sector, which accounts for approximately 71 per cent of total employment. This is largely due to the development of Edinburgh as a national and international administrative and tourist centre. In 1985, 230,000 people worked in Edinburgh and 3/4 of these – around 170,000 – were employed in the service sector. Only 17 per cent (under 40,000) of the city's employment is in manufacturing industry. Public sector activity accounted for 80,000 jobs in the city, reflecting Edinburgh's role as a capital city. In Scotland as a whole this figure is just over 60 per cent.

In the region as a whole manufacturing accounts for 19.7 per cent of employment and most of this is concentrated in the west, around Bathgate and Livingston. Unemployment here is well over 20 per cent and has been compounded in recent years by large scale closures, such as the British Leyland plant at Bathgate in 1984. The food and drink sector now accounts for almost a quarter of manufacturing employment, and electronics and electrical engineering are becoming increasingly important. East Lothian is predominantly a rural agricultural area and here unemployment remains relatively low.

Unemployment at February 1987 was 13.2 per cent, representing 48,637 people.

Local Authority Initiatives

The Regional Council supports a number of employment initiatives including community businesses, enterprise trusts, area initiatives and strategies for the unemployed. A Lothian Enterprise Board will be established in 1987. West Lothian District also has an active Economic Development Department.

See: *Lothian Region Structure Plan 1985, Report of Survey,* published by Planning Department, 1985.

Contact: Planning Department, Lothian Regional Council, George IV Bridge, Edinburgh, EH1 1UQ.

New Town

Livingston New Town was designated in 1962. Original population: 2,100, present population (31 March 1985): 40,380. The planned target population is 70,000. At March 1985, 15,045 people were employed in the town in 243 firms. Industrial floorspace covered 413,033 square metres and the housing stock was 14,210.

164

Science Park

Heriot-Watt University Research Park was established in 1972. At December 1986 it had 23 companies on 56 acres.

Scottish Development Agency

A range of initiatives including the Leith project, a regeneration project which the Agency managed up to May 1986, the Dunbar Initiative, and Bathgate Area Support for Enterprise (BASE) to regenerate the Bathgate area, in association with West Lothian District Council, Lothian Regional Council and Leyland Vehicles.

ORKNEY

Total Population ('000)			1981 18.4		1984 19.3		1985 19.3	

Main Districts
-
-

Age Structure 1985 ('000)	0–4 1.2	5–14 2.6	15–29 3.9	30–44 4.0	45–59/64 4.0	60/65–74 1.8	75+ 1.27

Unemployment Rates %	1981 9.4	1984 12.5	1985 11.6	1987 12.5

Average Earnings Male Female	1981 - -	1984 - -	1985 - -	1986 - -

Housing Completions	1981 112	1984 64	1985 24	1986

Industrial Floorspace ('000 sq. metres)	1981 -	1984 -	1985 -

Employment

Rateable Value 1986 £m.	Total 25.1	Domestic % 10.0	Commercial % 72.9	Industrial % 9.1	Other % 7.1

Local Authority Expenditure (£'000)	84/85 -	85/86 15,170	86/87 16,610e

- Figures not available
e Estimate
For notes on statistics see p. xi

Orkney is a group of islands to the north of the Scottish mainland and separated from it by seven miles of water known as the Pentland Firth. There are basically three groups of islands – the north isles, south isles, and a large island known as the mainland – which cover in total 97,581 hectares, and dotted around the islands are various historical and archaeological sites. Agriculture is the main activity with beef and dairy products being the principal products. Fishing is also important, along with boatbuilding, food processing, tourism, distilling, knitwear and crafts. Transport to the Scottish Mainland is available via Kirkwall Airport and ferry services to Scrabster and Aberdeen from Stromness. Kirkwall and Stromness are the two main towns.

Industry and Employment

Agriculture dominates the local economy, with 76,940.7 hectares given over to this use in the early 1980s. Approximately 1,754 people, out of a total population in 1985 of 19,000, work in fishing. Manufacturing accounts for only approximately 6.7 per cent of the workforce, with cheese-making, knitwear, distilling, food processing, and construction the major sectors. Construction has had a particularly bad time in recent years following the ending of construction work at the Flotta oil terminal. The terminal now employs about 500 people and handles 15 million tonnes of crude oil a year.

Unemployment at February 1987 was 12.5 per cent, representing 914 people.

Local Authority Initiatives

Provides sites and premises and finance is available from the Council's Reserve Fund.

See: *Orkney Economic Review,* regular, published by Chief Executives Department.

Contact: Economic Development Department, School Place, Kirkwall, KW15 1NY.

Highlands and Islands Development Board (HIDB)

Grants worth £1.1 million and loans of 581,000 were provided in 1985. Social development grants came to 34,000 and expenditure on specific Board projects amounted to £84,000.

SHETLAND

Total Population ('000)	1981	1984	1985
	22.7	23.3	23.4

Main Districts
-
-

Age Structure 1985 ('000)	0–4	5–14	15–29	30–44	45–59/64	60/65–74	75+
	1.6	3.5	5.1	5.3	4.2	1.6	1.28

Unemployment Rates %	1981	1984	1985	1987
	4.9	7.1	5.9	6.7

Average Earnings	1981	1984	1985	1986
Male	-	-	-	-
Female	-	-	-	-

Housing Completions	1981	1984	1985	1986
	191	73	97	-

Industrial Floorspace ('000 sq. metres)	1981	1984	1985
	-	-	-

Employment

Rateable Value 1986 £m.	Total	Domestic %	Commercial %	Industrial %	Other %
	66.4	4.6	10.2	79.5	5.4

Local Authority Expenditure (£'000)	84/85	85/86	86/87
	-	41,225	41,765e

- Figures not available
e Estimate
For notes on statistics see p. xi

The Shetlands is made up of over 100 islands, of which sixteen are inhabited and four have a bridge link to the mainland. The total land area is 143,268 hectares and the area is situated approximately 211 miles north of Aberdeen and 225 miles west of Bergen in Norway. Traditional industries are fishing, knitwear, agriculture, craft industries and tourism, but the industrial pattern of the area has been changed in recent years with the development of the North Sea oil industry. Shetland houses many of the land-based services associated with the Brent and Ninian oilfields and pipelines, and has the largest oil terminal in Europe at Sullom Voe. Lerwick, the main town, is the centre for most of the oil services. Agriculture is mainly based on small scale crofting. There are air and ferry links to Aberdeen and Edinburgh.

Industry and Employment

A large increase in the Shetland population took place between 1971 and 1981 as oil activity increased. In 1981 the population was 22,768, an increase of 29.4 per cent on the 1971 figure of 17,600. From 1981 to 1985, however, the population fell by 11 per cent to 20,264.

The workforce of the islands is between 10,000 and 11,000. Approximately 1,000 of these are employed in the primary industries of agriculture, fishing and quarrying and approximately 1,400 are employed in oil–related activities. A large temporary workforce was involved in the construction of the Sullom Voe oil terminal, reaching a peak of 7,000 workers in 1980/81, but this figure has declined substantially since then.

There are a number of fish processing plants around the islands and hand knitting is now being supplemented by machine knitted garments. The knitwear industry produces over £4 million worth of goods per annum and between 400,000 and 500,000 garments.

A recent study by GB Petroleum Consultants Ltd, for the Shetland Islands Council, forecasts the level of oil-related employment up to 1995. It notes that employment is likely to fall at the Sullom Voe and Sella Ness terminals as pipeline throughput and related tanker movements fall. However, employment is likely to increase on various marine service base sites and new employment will be created at the Dales Voe rig servicing base, which has yet to come into operation. From the above assumptions no major decline in employment is projected, with average employment levels remaining within 12 per cent to 15 per cent of current levels.

Unemployment is relatively low and at February 1987 was 6.7 per cent, representing 889 people.

Local Authority Initiatives

Provides serviced sites and premises and encourages oil-related growth while maintaining traditional industries.

See: *The Impact of Offshore Oil and Gas Related Activity on the Economic Development of the Shetland Islands,* published by GB Petroleum Consultants Ltd, 1986.

Shetland

Contact: Planning Department, Victoria Buildings, The Esplanade, Lerwick Shetlands ZE1 0LL

Highlands and Islands Development Board

Provides loan, equity and grant investment in the area.

STRATHCLYDE

Total Population ('000)	1981	1984	1985
	2,375.4	2,373.4	2,358.7

Main Districts			
Cunninghame	136.3	137.3	137.0
Glasgow	755.4	744.0	733.7
Hamilton	107.9	108.1	107.5
Kyle and Carrick	112.2	113.3	113.2
Monklands	109.8	109.3	108.1
Motherwell	149.4	149.7	149.1
Renfrew	205.3	203.9	203.4

Age Structure 1985 ('000)	0–4	5–14	15–29	30–44	45–59/64	60/65–74	75+
	153.5	313.0	592.1	445.7	527.4	196.5	129.7

Unemployment Rates %	1981	1984	1985	1987
	15.1	18.0	18.8	18.6

Average Earnings	1981	1984	1985	1986
Male	138.3	176.3	187.3	196.6
Female	84.8	111.4	119.1	129.7

Housing Completions	1981	1984	1985	1986
	7,253	6,580	6,943	–

Industrial Floorspace ('000 sq. metres)	1981	1984	1985
	–	–	–

Employment
Industrial Establishments 1987 = 5,800

Employees %	–100	100+	1,000+
	80.3	8.5	0.7

Rateable Value 1986 £m.	Total	Domestic %	Commercial %	Industrial %	Other %
	1,342.1	44.8	28.0	7.1	20.0

Local Authority Expenditure (£'000)	84/85	85/86	86/87
	–	1,418,429	1,501,838e

– Figures not available
e Estimate
For notes on statistics see p. xi

Strathclyde

The region contain almost half the population of Scotland within its area of 1,353,698 hectares and includes the most densely populated city in Scotland, Glasgow. The city is a major commercial centre and to its traditional industries of shipbuilding and engineering have been added newer industries such as light engineering, consumer goods production and oil-related services. There are a range of smaller towns surrounding Glasgow and the region also has a large amount of rural land including the Glencoe mountains, the isles of Mull, Bute and Arran and the farming areas of Ayrshire.

Industry and Employment

In June 1985 employment in the region stood at 800,000. This is 10,000 lower than the previous year's estimate and a fall of 184,000 or 19 per cent on the 1979 figure. The principal industries with declining employment, notably shipbuilding, steel, textiles, coalmining and heavy engineering, are well represented in the region and in the last fifteen years employment has fallen here much more rapidly than in Scotland as a whole. Manufacturing's share of employment in 1985 was estimated at 22.8 per cent representing 183,000 and involving a fall of 43 per cent on the 1979 figure of 323,000. Services on the other hand represented 67 per cent of all employment by 1985.

Population emigration has also been a problem and net emigration has been rising since 1981/82. In the four years between 1980/81 and 1983/84 net outward migration of 12,300 people took place: roughly 25 per cent were in the 25–34 age group and 20 per cent under 15.

Strathclyde has the highest regional unemployment rate in Scotland and the sixth highest in Great Britain. At February 1987 it was 18.6 per cent, representing 198,228 people.

Local Authority Initiatives

Thirteen 'areas of economic need' have been selected to be treated as Joint Economic Initiatives Areas involving the Regional Council, SDA and the district councils. Other policies aim to attract investment into former shipbuilding and steel making areas and develop training initiatives, support for community business, and support services for the unemployed.

See: *Strathclyde Economic Trends No. 13,* published by Chief Executives Department, 1986.

Contact: Chief Executives Department, 20 India Street, Glasgow, G2 4PF.

New Towns

Cumbernauld was designated in 1955. Original population: 3,000; present population (31 March 1986): 50,308. The planned target population is 70,000 and 60 per cent of the intake has come from Glasgow. Employment stands at 6,573 in 232 firms and industrial floorspace covers 416,380 square metres.

East Kilbride was designated in 1947. Original population: 2,400; present population (31 March 1986): 70,000. Target population is 82,500. 14,359 were employed in the town at March 1986 in 363 firms and manufacturing floorspace covered 690,680 square metres. Peel Park is a high-technology industrial campus in the town.

Irvine was designated in 1966. Original population: 34,600, present population (31 March 1986): 58,000; target population: 94,000. In March 1986, 111 firms had established on 213,999 square metres of floorspace.

Enterprise Zone

Clydebank Zone was established in 1981. It covers 270 hectares and in 1985 had 244 establishments, employing 5,800 people.

Science Park

West of Scotland Science Park was established in 1983 involving Glasgow and Strathclyde Universities and the SDA. At December 1986 there were fifteen firms on the 61.5-acre site.

Freeport

Freeport Scotland on thirty-five acres at Prestwick Airport became operational in September 1985. There are two firms on the site.

Scottish Development Agency

Involved in various initiatives in the region including the GEAR project in Glasgow's East End, the Clydebank project, the Motherwell project and the Inverclyde Initiative.

TAYSIDE

Total Population ('000)		1981 382.7	1984 394.4	1985 394.3	

Main Districts					
Angus		91.4	93.8	94.2	
Dundee		177.5	178.8	177.6	
Perth & Kinross		113.7	121.7	122.3	

Age Structure 1985 ('000)	0–4 23.7	5–14 49.5	15–29 93.1	30–44 74.0	45–59/64 89.4	60/65–74 36.2	75+ 27.6

Unemployment Rates %	1981 12.7	1984 15.2	1985 15.4	1987 15.4

Average Earnings		1981	1984	1985	1986
Male		127.2	162.4	172.1	179.5
Female		87.0	108.5	114.6	132.5

Housing Completions	1981 1,112	1984 1,386	1985 1,350	1986 –

Industrial Floorspace ('000 sq. metres)	1981 –	1984 –	1985 –

Employment				
Industrial Establishments	1987 = 1,160		
Employees %	–100 70.7	100+ 7.4	1,000+ 0.3

Rateable Value 1985 £m.	Total 229.7	Domestic % 45.0	Commercial % 25.2	Industrial % 6.6	Other % 23.0

Local Authority Expenditure (£'000)	84/85 –	85/86 210,628	86/87 220,204e

– Figures not available
e Estimate
For notes on statistics see p. xi

The region lies between the east coast of Scotland and the Central Highland belt and covers an area of 750,318 hectares. Often known as the region of rivers, Tayside has sparsely populated highland areas in the north and the industrial coastal belt. Agriculture is important and there are also significant areas of woodland. Industries include textiles, engineering, electronics, oil-related engineering companies, and consumer goods manufacture. The service sector is also increasing and the tourist industry is an important activity. Major towns are Dundee, Perth, Montrose, Arbroath and Kinross.

Industry and Employment

Approximately 24 per cent of the workforce are employed in manufacturing, 6 per cent in primary industries and 65 per cent in services. Services, however, have been increasing their share of employment as manufacturing employment falls.

Dundee, where approximately half the population of the region lives and works, is the industrial and commercial centre but it has suffered from the decline of traditional industries. It has been particularly dependent on large plant manufacturing, notably the jute industry, shipbuilding and food manufacture, all of which have declined in recent years. Textiles are still the biggest employer in the area, with approximately 5,000 jobs (4.5 per cent of the total). The growth in electronics and electrical engineering has partially offset the decline in traditional industries and has been accompanied by the growth in overseas-owned manufacturing plants. By 1984 there were 31 plants in the area, employing 7,300 people and representing 23 per cent of all manufacturing employment in the area, the second largest percentage of the Scottish regions.

Coupled with the decline of certain industries there has been a population fall. Between 1971 and 1981 the population fell by 2.2 per cent – Dundee lost 8.9 per cent of its population during this decade – and a further fall of 0.7 per cent occured between 1981 and 1985.

Unemployment at February 1987 was 15.4 per cent representing 27,309 people, although there are divergences throughout the region. Dundee and Arbroath have levels above 15 per cent but in Perth, where the service economy dominates, rates are much lower.

Local Authority Initiatives

Financial and other assistance to small/new firms etc. Business Development Area in Dundee (see below).

See: *Tayside Quarterly Economic Review*, published by Planning Department.

Contact: Planning Dept, Tayside House, Crichton Street, Dundee, DD1 1DJ.

Enterprise Zone

Tayside Enterprise Zone was designated in January 1984 on seven sites in Angus and Dundee districts. It covers 120 hectares and at 1985 had 24 establishments, employing 1,000 people.

Tayside

Scottish Development Agency (SDA)

Various initiatives including Scotland's first Business Development Area in the Blackness area of Dundee administered by the SDA and local authorities. Between 1982 and 1987 £120 million was invested in the area projects.

WESTERN ISLES

Total Population ('000)		1981	1984	1985	
		30.7	31.4	31.5	

Main Districts
-
-

Age Structure 1985 ('000)	0–4	5–14	15–29	30–44	45–59/64	60/65–74	75+
	1.8	4.7	6.5	5.6	6.5	2.7	2.7

Unemployment Rates %	1981	1984	1985	1987
	19.6	22.6	19.2	21.0

Average Earnings	1981	1984	1985	1986
Male	–	–	–	–
Female	–	–	–	–

Housing Completions	1981	1984	1985	1986
	247	32	137	

Industrial Floorspace ('000 sq. metres)	1981	1984	1985
	–	–	–

Employment

Rateable Value 1986 £m.	Total	Domestic %	Commercial %	Industrial %	Other %
	9.6	34.3	20.8	7.6	36.0

Local Authority Expenditure (£'000)	84/85	85/86	86/87
	–	28,461	30,650e

– Figures not available
e Estimate
For notes on statistics see p. xi

The Islands area covers a chain of islands lying north-north east to south-south west. At its closest it is about 30 miles and at its farthest about 60 miles from the north west coast of the mainland of Scotland. This chain, which is populated virtually throughout its length, is 130 miles long and covers an area of 7,717,381 hectares. The islands are close to important fishing grounds and to potential marine energy resources. Fishing is a major industry with herring historically the principal fishing resource. Tourism is on the increase and, because of its peripheral situation, the area is important as a location for defence and military installations. The main town is Stornaway on the island of Lewis, and there is an airport at Benbecula.

Industry and Employment

The population of the Western Isles is around 31,500, with Stornaway the major settlement. Over 8,000 people live in Stornaway and the total population of its

177

catchment area is around 21,000. The town is the centre of the Harris Tweed industry and a lively fishing port. More recently a new industry has been added to the area with the establishment of a heavy steel fabrication yard serving the offshore oil industry. Other industries include knitwear, construction, boatbuilding, craftwork and services.

The Higlands and Islands Development Board (HIDB) see fishing and fish processing as the main growth sectors in the long term, although outside Stornaway the smaller communities are dependent on largely part-time activities such as crofting, homeworking, knitting and tourism: approximately 77 per cent of the land is held in crofting tenure.

The population has remained relatively stable over recent years after a decrease between 1971 and 1981 of 0.9 per cent, but unemployment remains a serious problem. For most of the 1970s the Western Isles suffered one of the highest unemployment rates in Britain – in 1971 the rate of 22 per cent compared with a national average of 3.5 per cent and, although the rate fell in 1978 to around 11 per cent due to extensive participation in the government's job creation scheme and the establishment of Lewis Offshore in Stornaway, the rate has now risen to around 21 per cent, the highest in the UK.

At February 1987 it was 21 per cent, representing 2,062 people.

Local Authority Initiatives

Encourage indigenous enterprises and local initiatives. Sites and finance for industry.

See: *Western Isles Structure Plan: Draft Written Statement*, published by Planning Department, November 1986.

Contact: Planning Department, Sandwick Road, Stornaway, PA87 2BW

Highlands and Islands Development Board (HIDB)

HIDB finance and loans for the provision of workshops, or small factories, for manufacturing, craftwork or key trades in the islands.

Northern Ireland

NORTHERN IRELAND

Northern Ireland covers an area of 14,147 square kilometres and is divided into 26 district council areas. The major towns are Belfast in the east and Londonderry in the west. The area lacks many mineral sources (both coal and oil have to be imported) and, coupled with the small size of the local market, this has tended to favour concentration of industry and population on the eastern seaboard to provide trading links with rest of the UK. Traditional industries are in decline but aircraft manufacture has been relatively successful. Other industries include tobacco, vehicle components, oil-well equipment, electronic instruments, telecommunications equipment, carpets and synthetic rubber. Agriculture is also important and the province has large areas of natural beauty including the Mournes, the Antrim Glens, and the Fermanagh Lakeland. There are four major ports and regular air services to all parts of the UK.

Industry and Employment

Although the Northern Ireland population increased by only 1.7 per cent in the period 1971 to 1981, the potential workforce expanded much more rapidly. Between 1974 and 1979 the total working population increased by 11.1 per cent to 659,300, but remained broadly static thereafter, being 660,000 in 1984. The number of employees in manufacturing industry fell from 170,510 in 1974 to 144,950 in 1979 and was only 101,260 in 1984 – a decline of over 40 per cent over the decade.

In contrast, employment in services increased by 20.8 per cent between 1974 and 1979 to 317,800, and there was a smaller increase to 318,500 in 1984. While much of this expansion was concentrated in the public sector, private services also showed a sharp increase in employment over the past decade.

Further falls in manufacturing have occurred between 1984 and 1986 and the latest estimates, for June 1986, put total employment at 455,090, a fall of 7,330 on the previous year:

Employment levels

	June 1986	Change since last year
Agriculture[1]	9,260	+10
Energy and water	8,970	−10
Manufacturing	96,960	−4,110
Construction	20,360	−2,530
Services	319,540	−690
Total	455,090	−7,330

[1] not including self-employed

181

Northern Ireland

The situation in the manufacturing sector is patchy, however, and in a number of sectors output has risen while in others it has fallen. The strongest output performances have been in motor vehicles and other transport equipment sectors, and more recently in chemicals. Other sectors experiencing some recovery are leather, footwear, clothing, and paper and printing, while mechanical, electrical and instrument engineering, metal goods, food, textiles, timber and wood, and plastics and rubber have experienced falling output levels or no growth.

Agriculture, a major employer, has also been badly hit by poor weather conditions in recent years. For example, farming income for the 1985 calendar year at £67.4 million was some 48 per cent below the 1984 level and is the lowest in real terms since 1980.

Arising out of general economic trends and the rise in the area's working population, unemployment is now at 28 per cent and figures for the individual travel-to-work areas at February 1987 are as follows:

		Total Unemployed %
Ballymena	3,541	16.3
Belfast	63,737	18.7
Coleraine	7,618	27.5
Cookstown	2,772	37.1
Craigavon	11,726	21.5
Dungannon	4,056	30.9
Enniskillen	4,572	28.1
Londonderry	12,735	29.2
Magherafelt	2,992	30.0
Newry	7,810	33.0
Omagh	3,697	25.0
Strabane	3,968	39.2

New Towns

There are four new towns in Northern Ireland and in the early 1980s their populations were as follows:

Londonderry	80,816
Antrim	34,149
Ballymena	35,136
Craigavon	56,506

Enterprise Zones

There are two zones in Northern Ireland – Belfast and Londonderry.

Science Park

Belfast Science Park was established in November 1986 by Queens University, the University of Ulster and the Industrial Development Board for Northern Ireland. At December 1986 two firms were on site.

Industrial Development Board, Northern Ireland

Established in 1982 offering a range of incentives to industry and developing strategies for economic development. The Local Enterprise Development Unit (LEDU) promotes the development of small businesses, sectors etc.

Bibliography

This bibliography lists the principal sources of economic, industry population and employment data used in the preparation of this report.

Central government sources

Publications are available through HMSO, unless otherwise stated.

1981 Census publications

County Monitor Series, England and Wales, OPCS. Available from OPCS, St Catherine's House, 10 Kingsway, London, WC2B 6JP.

County Report Series, England and Wales, HMSO, two-volume reports for each county area.
Regional Bulletin Series, Scotland, General Register Office, Scotland. Series of summary reports on each region and island area in Scotland. Available from Customer Services, GRO, Ladywell House, Ladywell Road, Edinburgh, EH 12 7TF.
Regional Reports Series, Scotland, HMSO. Four-volume reports for each region and the islands areas grouped together.
Parliamentary Constituency Monitors, OPCS/GRO. Summary statistics available from above addresses in England and Scotland.
Ward and Parish Monitors, England and Wales, OPCS. Summary statistics available from above address in England.
European Assembly Constituency Monitors, United Kingdom (1974/1983 boundaries); OPCS/GRO.
Census 1981: Preliminary Report: England and Wales 1981, HMSO.
Census 1981, Scotland: Preliminary Report 1981, HMSO.
Census 1981: Preliminary Report, Northern Ireland, HMSO.
Census 1981: Key Statistics for Local Authorities, Great Britain, HMSO.

Census 1981: Preliminary Report for Towns, Urban and Rural Populations, England and Wales, HMSO.
Census 1981: Summary Report, Northern Ireland, HMSO. Includes data for each local government district.
Census 1981: Belfast Report, Northern Ireland, HMSO.
Census 1981: Historical Tables 1801–1981, England and Wales, HMSO.
Census 1981: Historical Tables 1801–1981, Scotland, HMSO.

*Specific topic reports including statistics by county, and sometimes new town and district level, include:

Census 1981: Sex, Age and Marital Status, Great Britain, HMSO.
Census 1981: Usual Residence, Great Britain, HMSO.
Census 1981: Regional Migration, England and Wales, HMSO, two volumes.
Census 1981: Scotland: Migration, HMSO, four volumes.
Census 1981: Migration Report: Northern Ireland, HMSO.
Census 1981: Economic Activity (microfiche), England and Wales, HMSO. Individual fiche for each county area.
Census 1981: Economic Activity (microfiche), Scotland, HMSO. Individual fiche for each region and island area.
Census 1981: Economic Activity, Northern Ireland, HMSO.
Geocode Index for Northern Ireland, HMSO. Employment analysis by grid references.
Census 1981: Workplace and Transport to Work, England and Wales, HMSO.
Census 1981: Scotland: Workplace and Transport to Work, HMSO.
Census 1981: Workplace and Transport to Work: Northern Ireland, HMSO.
Census 1981: New Towns Report, England and Wales, HMSO, two volumes.
Census 1981: Scotland: New Towns Report, HMSO.
Census 1981: Welsh Language in Wales, HMSO.

Small Area Statistics, (SAS): SAS are census statistics arranged by 'enumeration districts' (EDs). These EDs represents a group of 150 or so households. SAS, on magnetic tape or printed pages, can now be produced for the following local areas:

Enumeration Districts
District Electoral Wards
Local Government Districts
Counties (Regions in Scotland)
Civil Parishes (Communities in Wales)
Parliamentary Constituencies (1974 and 1983 boundaries)
European Assembly Constituencies
Urban Areas
New Towns
City Centres
Grid Squares
Regional Health Authorities
District Health Authorities

Bibliography

In addition, Scottish SAS are available for postcode sectors, employment exchange areas and regional electoral divisions.

For further details on SAS and for general inquiries on Census contact:

England and Wales: Census Customer Services, Titchfield, Fareham, Hampshire, PO15 5RR.

Scotland: Census Customer Services, General Register Office, Ladywell House, Ladywell Road, Edinburgh, EH12 7TF.

Northern Ireland: General Register Office, Oxford House, 49–55 Chichester Street, Belfast, BT1 4HP.

OTHER POPULATION STATISTICS

OPCS Monitor Series PP1, annual, OPCS. Mid-year population estimates for counties, districts, regions. Available from OPCS, St Catherine's House, 10 Kingsway, London, WC2B 6JP.
Annual Estimates of the Population of Scotland, GRO. Available from GRO, Ladywell House, Ladywell Road, Edinburgh, EH12 7TF.
Annual Report of the Registrar General for Scotland, HMSO.
Annual Report of the Registrar Gereral for Northern Ireland, HMSO.
OPCS Monitor VS Vital Statistics: Local and Health Areas, HMSO.
The Four-Weekly Vital Statistics Return of the Registrar General, Scotland, HMSO.
Registrar General's Quarterly Return for Northern Ireland, HMSO.
OPCS Monitor Series PP3, annual OPCS. Gives projections for counties, districts, and boroughs in England. Available from above address.
Home Population Projections for the Counties of Wales, annual, Welsh Office. Available from E & SS Division, Welsh Office, Cathays Park, Cardiff, CF1 3NQ.
Projected Population of Scotland, annual, GRO. Available from above address.
Population Trends, quarterly, HMSO. General statistics plus special topics on local statistics.

EMPLOYMENT/UNEMPLOYMENT

Employment Gazette, monthly, HMSO. Monthly unemployment figures by county, region, parliamentary constituency, travel to work areas plus the main results from the Census of Employment.
Business Monitor PA 1003: Size Analyses of UK Businesses, annual, HMSO. Includes a table for individual counties covering number of firms by employment size bands and total number of employees.
Department of Economic Development, Northern Ireland Press Notice, regular.

186

HOUSING

Local Housing Statistics, England and Wales, quarterly, HMSO.
Scottish Housing Statistics, annual, HMSO.
Welsh Housing Statistics, annual, Welsh Office. Available from E & SS Division, Welsh Office.
Housing and Construction Statistics, annual, HMSO. Gives some figures for regions and metropolitan counties in England, Wales, and Scotland.
Housing Press Notice, regular, DoE. Gives data every quarter for starts and completions in local authority areas, new towns and housing association areas plus improvements, conversions etc.

EARNINGS/INCOME

New Earnings Survey, Part E – Analyses by Region and Age Group, annual, HMSO.
The Survey of Personal Incomes, annual, HMSO. Some figures on incomes and tax by counties in England and Wales, regions of Scotland, and Northern Ireland.

INDUSTRIAL AND COMMERCIAL FLOORSPACE

Commercial and Industrial Floorspace Statistics, England, annual, HMSO, 1982–85, ceased publication 1986.
Commercial and Industrial Floorspace Statistics, Wales, annual, Welsh Office. Available from E & SS Division, Welsh Office.

OTHER SUBJECT AREAS

General Titles

Regional Trends, annual, HMSO. Includes a regional profile section giving basic data on county areas in England and Wales, regions in Scotland and Northern Ireland.
Scottish Abstract of Statistics, annual, HMSO.
Digest of Welsh Statistics, annual, Welsh Office. Available from E & SS Division, Welsh Office.
Northern Ireland Annual Abstract of Statistics, annual, HMSO.
Scottish Economic Bulletin, twice yearly, HMSO.

Specialized Titles

Agricultural Statistics, annual, HMSO
Welsh Agricultural Statistics, annual, Welsh Office. Available from E & SS Division, Welsh Office.

Bibliography

Agriculture Scotland, annual, HMSO.

Economic Report on Scottish Agriculture, annual, HMSO.

Statistical Review of Northern Ireland Agriculture, annual, Department of Agriculture for Northern Ireland. Available from Economic and Statistics Division, Department of Agriculture for Northern Ireland, Dundonald House, Belfast, BT4 3SB.

Transport Statistics, Great Britain, annual, HMSO. Gives vehicle registration by county, region, and Northern Ireland.

Scottish Transport Statistics, annual, Scottish Office. Available from Scottish Office Library, Room 2/64, New St Andrew's House, St James Centre, Edinburgh, EH1 3TD.

Some other central government publications contain selected tables on county areas. For information on these, use the *Guide to Official Statistics*, 1986, HMSO.

LOCAL AUTHORITY PUBLICATIONS

Publications consulted or noted in the preparation of this report. For more detailed publications lists please consult individual local authorities direct. All publications are produced by the relevant County Council unless otherwise stated.

AVON

Avon Economic Review, Planning Department, 1985.

Avon Economic Statistics, Planning Department, 1984.

Avon County Structure Plan: First Alteration – Written Statement – incorporating memorandum, housing, transport and employment policies, Public Relations and Publicity, January 1986.

BEDFORDSHIRE

Economic Development – A Policy Review, Employment Committee, November 1985.

BERKSHIRE

Development Trends in Berkshire, Planning Department, March 1986.

See also: *Economic Growth and Planning Policies in the South East*, Housing Research Foundation, November 1986.

BUCKINGHAMSHIRE

Buckinghamshire County Structure Plan: monitoring report – key statistics 1985, Planning Department, December 1985.

See also: *Economic Growth and Planning Policies in the South East*, Housing Research Foundation, November 1986.

CAMBRIDGESHIRE

Fenland Rural Development Area: Strategy and Work Programme for 1987/88, Planning and Research Department, October 1986.
East Anglia Regional Commentary 1985/86, East Anglia Consultative Committee, March 1986.

CHESHIRE

Cheshire County Structure Plan – Explanatory Memorandum and Written Statement, Planning Department, 1986.
Employment and Industry in Cheshire: Progress in the 1970s and prospects for the future, Planning Department, 1986.
Cheshire Current Facts and Figures, monthly, Research and Intelligence Section.

CLEVELAND

Cleveland, 1986–1990, an Economic, Demographic and Social Review, Research and Intelligence, June 1986.
Cleveland Structure Plan, Discussion Paper: People and Jobs, Planning Department, March 1986.
Cleveland Structure Plan, Discussion Paper: Economy. Planning Department, November 1986.
Cleveland Review 1974–84, Monitoring Report, Planning Department, February 1985.
Employment and Unemployment in Cleveland – A Presentation of the Available Data, Research and Intelligence, February 1986.
Labour Market Information Survey, Research and Intelligence, August 1984.
Cleveland County Council – Economic Initiatives, Research and Intelligence, undated.
Regional Development Grants and Investment in Manufacturing Industry, Research and Intelligence, February 1986.
Manufacturing Employment Change in Cleveland, 1976–1981, Planning Department, May 1985.
Economic Development and New Technology in Cleveland, Research and Intelligence, August 1985.
Employment Review, quarterly, Planning Department.

CORNWALL

Economic Policies and Programmes, Planning Department, 1986.
Cornwall Structure Plan: Project Report, Planning Department, 1985.
Cornwall Structure Plan, 1st Alteration – Discussion Paper: Employment and Industry, Planning Department, October 1985.
Cornwall and the Isles of Scilly, Rural Development Programme, Planning Department, 1985.

Bibliography

CUMBRIA

Looking for Jobs – an Employment Development Strategy for Cumbria, Economic Development Department, January 1987.
Employment Forecasts. Technical Note 2, Planning Department, 1986.
Housing Projections. Technical Note 3, Planning Department, 1986.
Joint Rural Development Programme for Cumbria. Submission 1987–1990, Planning Department, October 1986.
Cumbria and Lake District Joint Structure Plan/Proposals report: first alteration and roll forward to 1996, Planning Department, 1986.
Cumbria Monitor, monthly, Planning Department.

DERBYSHIRE

Economic Development Monitoring Report, quarterly, Planning Department.
Unemployment in Derbyshire, Planning Department, July 1986.
Economic Development in Shire Counties, Case Study 1. Derby and Derbyshire, CLES, March 1987.

DEVON

Employment in Devon: Policies and Programmes, Engineering and Planning Department, 1986.
County Structure Plan: First alteration: Written Statement, Engineering and Planning Department, 1985.
County Structure Plan: First alteration: Explanatory Memorandum, Engineering and Planning Department, 1985.
Devon in figures, annual, Treasurer's Department.

DORSET

Dorset Data, Planning Department, 1986.

DURHAM

Manufacturing Employment change in County Durham since 1965, Planning Department, 1986.
County Structure Plan: County Durham 1986, Planning Department, 1986.
A Future for the Durham Dales: Policy Document, Planning Department, 1986.

EAST SUSSEX

The East Sussex Economy – Employment Review, Planning Department, 1985.
Greater Brighton Area: Employers' Survey, Planning Department, December 1985.

190

ESSEX

Employment Monitoring Report, Planning Department, March 1986.
Essex Structure Plan: Proposed Alteration, Planning Department, August 1986.

GLOUCESTERSHIRE

Economic Development Strategy – Programme for Action, Planning Department, September 1986.
The South Forest Rural Development Area: Annual Review of Progress and Work Programme, 1987/88, Planning Department, October 1986.

GREATER LONDON

Annual Abstract of Greater London Statistics, 1984–85, GLC, 1986.
The London Industrial Strategy, GLC, 1985.
The London Labour Plan, GLC, 1986.
A City Divided, London Strategic Policy Unit, 1986.

GREATER MANCHESTER

Structure Plan Policies Approved by the Secretary of State as at January 1986, Planning Department, 1986.
A Strategy for Employment, Economic Development Unit (Manchester City Council), 1987.
Major Industrial Developments in Greater Manchester in 1984, Planning Department, 1985.
Comparative Study of Conurbations: Urban Change in Greater Manchester, Planning Departments, 1985
Local Unemployment in Greater Manchester: Analysis by Age and Duration, 1985.
Local Unemployment in Greater Manchester: Analysis by Sex, Planning Department, 1985.
Greater Manchester – The Facts, Greater Manchester Economic Development Corporation, 1986.

HAMPSHIRE

Hampshire Strategic Monitoring Report, Planning Department, 1986.
Hampshire Facts and Figures, Planning Department, 1986.
Hampshire County Council's Support for the Economy, Planning Department, 1986.
Industrial Land Supply, Planning Department, 1986.
High Technology Industry in Hampshire, Planning Department, 1984.
Employment Newsletter, regular, Planning Department.

Bibliography

HEREFORD AND WORCESTER

Hereford and Worcester County Structure Plan: approved written statement, Planning Department, 1985.

HERTFORDSHIRE

Hertfordshire County Structure Plan: Written Statement, Planning Department, May 1986.
Hertfordshire County Structure Plan: Explanatory Memorandum, Planning Department, 1986.
See also: Economic Growth and Planning Policies in the South East, Housing Research Foundation, November 1986.

HUMBERSIDE

A Strategy and Programme for Economic Development, Economic Development Unit, April 1986.
Humberside Facts and Figures 1986, Economic Development Unit, 1986.
Humberside Employment Monitor, six issues a year, Economic Development Unit.

ISLE OF WIGHT

See: Regional Trends in the South East. 1985-86, SERPLAN, May 1986.

KENT

Kent Economic Development Review, Planning Department, October, 1985.

LANCASHIRE

The Lancashire Clothing Industry, Planning Department, October 1985.
Structure and Performance of Manufacturing Industry in Lancashire, 1980-82, Planning Department, October 1985.
The Lancashire Structure Plan: Explanatory Memorandum, Planning Department, 1986.
Lancashire 1986: An Economic Situation Report, Planning Department, 1986.
Lancashire Rural Development Programme 1987/88, Planning Department, October 1986.

LEICHESTERSHIRE

Review of the Leicestershire Economy, Planning Department, June 1986.
Leicestershire Structure Plan alteration No. 2: Written Statement, Planning Department, March 1985.
Leicestershire Structure Plan alteration No. 2: Explanatory Memorandum, Planning Department, March 1985.

LINCOLNSHIRE

Lincolnshire Structure Plan, written statement, Planning Department.

MERSEYSIDE

Merseyside Economic Prospect, quarterly, Liverpool Research Group in Macroeconomics, Liverpool University.
Liverpool's Economy, Employment and Unemployment: Changes and Trends 1978–1991, Planning Department (City of Liverpool), 1985.

NORFOLK

Norfolk Structure Plan: Explanatory Memorandum and Written Statement, Planning Department, April 1986.
Norfolk Structure Plan: Seventh Monitoring Report, Planning Department, December 1986.
East Anglia Regional Commentary 1985/86, East Anglia Consultative Committee, March 1986.

NORTHAMPTONSHIRE

Northamptonshire Replacement County Structure Plan, Planning Department, June 1986.
Northamptonshire Replacement County Structure Plan: Industry and Commerce Provision, Background Paper, Planning Department, June 1986.
Industrial Land Development Programme 1986/87, Planning Department, November 1986.

NORTHUMBERLAND

Jobs in Northumberland – Employment and Unemployment Trends, Employment Sub-Committee, 1985.
County Council Employment Initiatives, Employment Sub-Committee, 1985.

Bibliography

NORTH YORKSHIRE

Fifth Annual Review of the Economic Development Strategy, Industrial Development Unit, 1986.
Joint Rural Development Programme for North Yorkshire: Work Programme 1986–89, Planning Department, December 1985.

NOTTINGHAMSHIRE

Nottinghamshire Structure Plan – Second Monitoring Report, Planning Department, 1985.
Economic Development in Shire Counties, Case Study 2: Nottingham and Nottinghamshire, CLES, January 1987.

OXFORDSHIRE

See: Economic Growth and Planning Policies in the South East, Housing Research Foundation, November 1986.

SHROPSHIRE

Shropshire County Structure Plan: Alteration No. 1: Written Statement, Planning Department, December 1984.
Shropshire County Structure Plan: Alteration No. 1: Explanatory Memorandum, Planning Department, December 1984.

SOMERSET

Economic Development in Somerset: Position statement and Review of Possible Further Policy options, Economic Development Unit, 1985.
Somerset Structure Plan, first alteration: Discussion Paper on Economic Change, Planning Department, 1984.
West Somerset Rural Development Area Programme, 1986–89, Planning Department January 1986.
Industrial Land and Buildings in Somerset, Second Review and Programme, 1986–87, Planning Department, 1985.

SOUTH YORKSHIRE

South Yorkshire Statistics, annual (up to abolition in 1986), Chief Executives Department, South Yorkshire County Council.

Working it out – an outline Employment Plan for Sheffield, Employment and Economic Development Department, 1987.

STAFFORDSHIRE

Staffordshire Structure Plan – Explanatory Memorandum, Planning Department, 1982.
Economic Development in Shire Counties, Case Study No.3: Stoke and Staffordshire, CLES, January 1987.

SUFFOLK

Suffolk Towards 2000: County Structure Plan: Explanatory Memorandum to the Proposed Alterations, Planning Department, September 1986.
Rural Development Programme 1987–88, Planning Department, November 1986.
East Anglia Regional Commentary 1985/86, East Anglia Consultative Committee, March 1986.

SURREY

Economic Growth and Planning Policies in the South East, Housing Research Foundation, November 1986.

TYNE AND WEAR

Structure Plan Annual Report, annual (up to abolition in 1986), Planning Department, Tyne and Wear County Council.
Economic Development Bulletin, regularly (up to abolition in 1986), Planning Department, Tyne and Wear County Council.
Tyne and Wear in Crisis. North East Trade Union Studies Information Unit, 1985.

WARWICKSHIRE

Warwickshire Structure Plan, Progress and Information Report, Planning Department, November 1985.
Warwickshire Structure Plan Review, Explanatory Memorandum, Planning Department, 1984.
Warwickshire Unemployment Report, regular, Planning Department.

WEST MIDLANDS

West Midlands Economy in 1984, West Midlands CC (now abolished), 1985.
Statistics, annual (up to 1985), West Midlands CC.

Bibliography

West Midlands Regional Strategy Review, Paper No.4: Employment and Economic Regeneration, West Midlands CC, February 1985.
Future Employment Prospects for the West Midlands County, West Midlands CC, November 1984.
Economic Briefing, regular, West Midlands Enterprise Board.

Most of the County Council reports and other sector reports can be obtained from the West Midlands Enterprise Board.

WEST SUSSEX

Interview Survey of Employers, Planning Department, June 1986.
West Sussex – Well worth Living and Working In, CBI Response to 1986 County Council Interview Survey of Employers, Confederation of British Industry, March 1987.
See also: Economic Growth and Planning Policies in the South East, Housing Research Foundation, November 1986.

WEST YORKSHIRE

Economic Trends, quarterly (up to abolition in 1986), Planning Department.
Economic Bulletin, monthly (up to abolition in 1986), Planning Department.
Rural Development Programme – Pennine Rural Development Area, West Yorkshire, Pennine RDA Strategy Committee, December 1984.
Prospects for the West Yorkshire Coalfield, Planning Department, December 1984.
See also: Turning the Corner–A Strategy for the Yorkshire and Humberside Region, Yorkshire and Humberside Councils Association, 1985.

WILTSHIRE

Western Wiltshire Structure Plan Explanatory Memorandum, Planning Department, 1985.
Employment, Land and Floorspace, Planning Department, October 1986.

CLWYD

Abstract of Statistics, annual, Chief Executives Department.

DYFED

County Structure Plan, Written Statement, Planning Department.

GWENT

Economic Progress Report, quarterly. Planning Department.

MID-GLAMORGAN

Economic and Social Conditions in Mid-Glamorgan, Economic Policy and Research Unit, February 1986.

WEST GLAMORGAN

Economic Development in Shire Counties, Case Study No. 4: Swansea and West Glamorgan, CLES, January 1987.

BORDERS

Economic Development – Annual Report 1985, Planning and Development Department, 1986.
Pilot Rural Development Areas Study, Planning and Development, October 1986.

CENTRAL

Information Bulletin, regular, Planning Department.

DUMFRIES AND GALLOWAY

Dumfries and Galloway Structure Plan, Written Statement, Planning Department, undated.
A Study of Forest Resources and Related Industry, Economic Development, 1986.

FIFE

Strategic Projections 5, Economic Development and Planning Department, July 1986.

GRAMPIAN

Strategic Forecasts: Employment, Population, Housing, 1986 Update, Physical Planning Department, August 1986.

Bibliography

Future Oil and Gas Prospects, Physical Planning Department, June 1986.
Quarterly Economic Review, Physical Planning Department, annual subscription.
Annual Report on Unemployment, Physical Planning Department, November 1986.
Grampian Region Structure Plan, Aberdeen Area Review Survey 1985, Physical Planning Department, 1985.
Grampian Region Structure Plan, Rural Area, Report of Survey and Supplementary Volume, Physical Planning Department, 1984.

HIGHLANDS

Highlands and Islands Development Board, Annual Report, HIDB, 1986.
Rural Scotland Price Survey, half-yearly, Higlands and Islands Development Board.

LOTHIAN

Lothian Region Structure Plan 1985: Report of Survey, Planning Department, July 1985.

ORKNEYS

Orkney Economic Review, regular, Chief Executives Department.

SHETLANDS

The Impact of Offshore Oil and Gas related Activity on the Economic Development of the Shetland Islands, Planning Department, 1986.
Shetland: Economy and Industry 1982/83, Research and Development Department, 1985.

STRATHCLYDE

Strathclyde Economic Trends, quarterly, Chief Executives Department.
Stratchlyde Structure Plan: Monitoring Report, Physical Planning Department, 1987.
Stratchlyde Structure Plan: Update Written Statement, Physical Planning Department, 1987.

TAYSIDE

Tayside Quarterly Economic Review, quarterly, Planning Department.

WESTERN ISLES

Western Isles Structure Plan: Draft Written Statement, Planning and Development Department, November 1986.

NORTHERN IRELAND

The Northern Ireland Economy: Review and Prospects, annual, Coopers and Lybrand.
Northern Ireland Economic Council, Annual Report, NIEC, October 1986.

NEW TOWNS

Report of the Development Corporations, annual, HMSO.
Report of the Development Corporations (Scotland), annual, HMSO.
Report of the Cwmbran Development Corporation, annual, HMSO.
Report of the Commission for the New Towns, annual, HMSO.
Britain's New Towns, annual, special feature, usually in October, November or December issue of *Town and Country Planning*.

DEVELOPMENT AGENCIES

Annual Report, Scottish Development Agency.
Annual Report, Welsh Development Agency.
Annual Report, Highlands and Islands Development Board.
Mid-Wales: Annual Report, Development Board for Rural Wales.
Annual Report, Development Commission.

CIPFA STATISTICAL PUBLICATIONS

Local Government Comparative Statistics, annual.
Local Government Trends, annual.
Finance and General Statistics, annual.
Rating Review Estimates of Income and Expenditure, Summary Volume, annual, Scottish Branch.

For details of CIPFA's range of statistics contact CIPFA, 3 Robert Street, London, WC2N 6BH.

OTHER PUBLICATIONS

Great Britain Industrial Statistics, Employee Analysis, twice a year, Market Location Ltd.

199

Bibliography

Science Park Directory, United Kingdom Science Park Association, 1986.

Enterprise Zone Information, 1984–85, HMSO, 1986.

The Freeport Experiment, Adam Smith Institute, 1986.

Mind Your Local Business, Eurofi (UK) Ltd, 1986. Useful guide to the range of information sources on local areas. Covers a number of sources not included in this review, e.g. property consultants, chambers of commerce, general consultants etc.

SELECTED BIBLIOGRAPHICAL/ABSTRACTING SERVICES

Bibliographical services covering local authority and related documents include the following:

Urbandoc News, monthly, Capital Planning Information, annual subscription. Concentrates on publications from central government departments and local authorities. CPI, The Grey House, Broad Street, Stamford, Lincolnshire PE9 1PR.

Urban Abstracts, monthly, Research Library, London Research Centre, annual subscription. Mainly abstracts of research reports and journal articles but includes local authority publications. Also available online through *ACOMPLINE* and *URBALINE*. Research Library, Room 514, County Hall, London, SE1 7PB.

Planning Information Digest and Economic Development Digest, monthly, Planning Exchange, annual subscriptions. Abstracts of local authority, central government, EEC and other material. Planning Exchange, 186 Bath Street, Glasgow, G2 4HG.

Local Economic News, monthly, Centre for Local Economic Strategies, annual subscription. Abstracts of local authority reports and other material relating specifically to local economic policies and strategies. CLES, Heron House, Brazernose Street, Manchester, M2 5HD.

SELECTED LIBRARIES/INFORMATION SERVICES

The following are useful sources of central government statistics:

Statistics and Market Intelligence Library, 1 Victoria Street, London, SW1H OET. Also takes a few local authority publications.

Official Publications Library, The British Library, Great Russell Street, London, WC1B 3DG (Tel: 01-636-1544). Please telephone before calling at the library.

Business Information Service, University of Warwick Library, Coventry, CV4 7AL. Commercial information service based on large collection of UK and international statistics.

The library, OPCS, St Catherine's House, 10 Kingsway, London, WC2B 6JP. Census material and related population statistics. The library is open to the general public but space is limited and prior booking is recommended, and is essential when use is to be made of the Small Area Statistics.

Other libraries containing significant collections of local authority material include:

The British Library Lending Division, Boston Spa, Wetherby, Yorks.

Department of the Environment Library, 2 Marsham Street, London, SW1P 3EB. Collection of structure plan and local plan documents for England and Wales. Written permission to use the library must be obtained.

Research Library, London Research Centre, 5th Floor, Main Building, County Hall, London. Large collection covering all aspects of local government activities. Available to London local authorities. Others should contact the Librarian.

The Library, the Planning Exchange, 186 Bath Street, Glasgow, G2 4HG. Central collection of Scottish local government publications, and some English and Welsh publications. Members of the Planning Exchange have access to the library and information services. Other users should contact the library for details.

The Library, Centre for Local Economic Strategies, Heron House, Brazennose Street, Manchester, M2 5HD. Collection of local authority documents, research reports and articles on local economic initiatives. Members of CLES have access. Others should contact the Information Officer.